THE MYTHOS
Of
American
Exceptionalism

"When Fascism comes to America; It will come wrapped in the flag and carrying a cross."

Sinclair Lewis

1.

Once upon a time in America, at least those of us of a certain age can remember, saying the Pledge of Allegiance almost first thing in school. From there, we were taught about how great America is. Not only that we were taught that America was the greatest country that ever existed, currently exists, or will ever exist. Yes, we were slowly and methodically being indoctrinated into the philosophy of American Exceptionalism.

Now don't get me wrong, I'm proud to be an American. Every time the National Anthem is played, I stand, place my hand over my heart and think of all the men and women who made the ultimate sacrifice for me to do this. But then that is where is my belief in American Exceptionalism ends and my questioning begins. Especially when we have a President saying that he going to, "Make America Great Again." When was America ever great? I am genuinely curious as to the response. And for those who like to say, "America, if you don't like it, leave!" Hear me out. It pays to question these things. Just as important as being well read on your American and world history. I know, I just said the one word that makes most Americans cringe, "Read." Because reading takes effort, and it takes time. We much rather have someone tell us how to think rather than develop our own thoughts.

That is hopefully what this book is going to investigate. The myth of American Exceptionalism. I have done extensive research into this topic and am very excited to share with you my discoveries. Naturally, as with most of my writings, it is going to be viewed favorably by some, and not so favorably by others. By all means, **do not shoot the messenger.**

What we have now in this country is mass polarization, pretty much divided along educational and religious lines. Those with less education tend to be more religious and also lends themselves to lean conservative. So, we, as Americans think we know what American Exceptionalism is, but what exactly is it in terms of the observation of others?

According to the observations of others, the theory that America is qualitatively different from other nations. For the ideology that America has an exceptional mission in the world,

The German professor Sieglinde Lemke argued that the Statue of Liberty "signifies this proselytizing mission as the natural extension of the US' sense of itself as an exceptional nation."

American exceptionalism is a European-born critique of the United States of America that the country sees its history as inherently different from that of other nations, stemming from its emergence from the American Revolution, becoming what the political scientist Seymour Martin Lipset called "the first new nation" and developing a uniquely American ideology, "Americanism", based on liberty, equality before the law, individual responsibility, republicanism, representative democracy, and laissez-faire economics. This ideology itself is often referred to as "American exceptionalism." Second is the idea that America has a unique mission to transform the world. President Abraham Lincoln stated in the Gettysburg address (1863) during the American Civil War, in reference to the preservation of the United States itself, Americans have a duty to ensure, "government of the people, by the people, for the people, shall not perish from the earth." Third is the sense that America's history and its mission give it a superiority over other nations.

The theory of the exceptionalism of the U.S. has developed over time and can be traced to many sources. French political scientist and historian Alexis de Tocqueville was the first writer to describe the country as "exceptional" in 1831 and 1840. The actual phrase "American exceptionalism" was originally coined by the Soviet leader Joseph Stalin in 1929 as a critique of a revisionist faction of American communists that argued that the American political climate was unique and made it an 'exception' to certain elements of Marxist theory. U.S. president Ronald Reagan is often credited with having crystallized that ideology in recent decades.

Political scientist Eldon Eisenach argues that American exceptionalism in the 21st century has come under attack from the postmodern left as a reactionary myth: "The absence of shared purpose is ratified in the larger sphere of liberal-progressive public philosophy. Beginning with the assumption of American exceptionalism as a reactionary myth".

Now, given the fact that the American political landscape is fairly well split evenly between conservatives and progressives, the conservative movement has pretty much claimed the mantle of Exceptionalism as their own. By doing so, they could automatically paint anyone who did not believe in said exceptionalism was somehow Unamerican. Of course, nothing but could be further from the truth, but it is the *appearance* they sought to show to discredit their opposition and silence any dissent. Well played, right wing. Well played. In fact, the phrase fell to obscurity after the 1930s until American newspapers popularized it in the 1980s to describe America's cultural and political uniqueness. The phrase became an issue of contention between the presidential candidates Barack Obama and John McCain in the 2008 presidential campaign, with McCain attacking Obama for allegedly disbelieving the concept.

The first reference to the concept by name, and possibly its origin, was by the French writer Alexis de Tocqueville in his 1835/1840 work Democracy in America: The position of the Americans is therefore quite exceptional, and it may be believed that no democratic people will ever be placed in a similar one. Their strictly Puritanical origin, their exclusively commercial habits, even the country they inhabit, which seems to divert their minds from the pursuit of science, literature, and the arts, the proximity of Europe, which allows them to neglect these pursuits without relapsing into barbarism, a thousand special causes, of which I have only been able to point out the most important, have singularly concurred to fix the mind of the American upon purely practical objects. His passions, his wants, his education, and everything about him seem to unite in drawing the native of the United States earthward; his religion alone bids him turn, from time to time, a transient and distracted glance to heaven. Let us cease, then, to view all democratic nations under the example of the American people. Newspaper reporting the annexation of the Republic of Hawaii in 1898. American exceptionalism has fueled American expansion through the ideology of manifest destiny.

Kammen says that many foreign visitors commented on American exceptionalism including Karl Marx, Francis Lieber, Hermann Eduard von Holst, James Bryce, H. G. Wells, G. K. Chesterton, and Hilaire Belloc and that they did so in complimentary terms. The theme became common, especially in textbooks. From the 1840s to the late 19th century, the McGuffey Readers sold 120 million copies and were studied by most American students. Skrabec (2009) argues the Readers "hailed American exceptionalism, manifest destiny, and America as God's country.... Furthermore, McGuffey saw America as having a future mission to bring liberty and democracy to the world."

In June 1927 Jay Lovestone, a leader of the Communist Party USA and who would be soon named as general secretary, described America's economic and social uniqueness. He noted the increasing strength of American capitalism and the country's "tremendous reserve power" and said that both prevented a communist revolution. In 1929, the Soviet leader Joseph Stalin, disbelieving that America was so resistant to revolution, called Lovestone's ideas "the heresy of American exceptionalism," which was the first use of the specific term "American exceptionalism." The Great Depression appeared to underscore Stalin's argument that American capitalism falls under the general laws of Marxism. In June 1930, during the national convention of the Communist Party USA in New York, it was declared, "The storm of the economic crisis in the United States blew down the house of cards of American exceptionalism and the whole system of opportunistic theories and illusions that had been built upon American capitalist 'prosperity.'"

In general, Americans have had consideration in national "uniqueness." The historian Dorothy Ross points to three different currents regarding unique characteristics. Some Protestants believed American progress would facilitate the return of Jesus Christ and the Christian Millennium. Some 19th century historians linked American liberty to the development of liberty in Anglo-Saxon England. Other American writers looked to the "millennial newness" of America. Henry Nash Smith stressed the theme of "virgin land" in the American frontier that promised an escape from the decay that had befallen to earlier republics.

Recently, socialists and other writers tried to discover or describe this exceptionalism of the U.S. within and outside its borders. The concept has also been discussed in the context of the 21st century in a book co-authored by U.S. Vice President Dick Cheney: Exceptional: Why the World Needs a Powerful America (2015).

While America may or may not be exceptional, one thing is for certain, America is the 800-pound gorilla and where does an 800-pound gorilla sleep? Anywhere it wants.

2.

Now for the next few chapters, I would like to discuss some of the myths of American Exceptionalism. While there are many myths and shortcomings, I have decided to limit my discourses to just five of the biggest or major myths. So, without any further ado, let's begin.

#1.) God Is on Our Side.

A crucial component of American exceptionalism is the belief that the United States has a divinely ordained mission to lead the rest of the world. Ronald Reagan told audiences that there was "some divine plan" that had placed America here, and once quoted Pope Pius XII saying, "Into the hands of America God has placed the destinies of an afflicted mankind." Bush offered a similar view in 2004, saying, "We have a calling from beyond the stars to stand for freedom." The same idea was expressed, albeit less nobly, in Otto von Bismarck's alleged quip that "God has a special providence for fools, drunks, and the United States." Also, let us not forget George W. Bush's infamous quote that the United States was now on "a crusade" against those who perpetrated the attacks on 9/11, who were Arabic. Perhaps it was a poor choice of words or a deliberate reminder to the Arabs that the white Europeans were coming for the…Again. Of course, history tells us what has happened and will happen in the future. Hint: The Arabs win, as throughout history they have been fighting and if they have no one to fight they will fight each other.

Confidence is a valuable commodity for any country. But when a nation starts to think it enjoys the mandate of heaven and becomes convinced that it cannot fail or be led astray by scoundrels or incompetents, then reality is likely to deliver a swift rebuke. Ancient Athens, Napoleonic France, imperial Japan, and countless other countries have succumbed to this sort of hubris, and nearly always with catastrophic results.

Despite America's many successes, the country is hardly immune from setbacks, follies, and boneheaded blunders. If you have any doubts about that, just reflect on how a decade of ill-advised tax cuts, two costly and unsuccessful wars, and a financial meltdown driven mostly by greed and corruption have managed to squander the privileged position the United States enjoyed at the end of the 20th century. Instead of assuming that God is on their side, perhaps Americans should heed Abraham Lincoln's admonition that our greatest concern should be "whether we are on God's side."

Given the many challenges Americans now face, from persistent unemployment to the burden of winding down two deadly wars, it's unsurprising that they find the idea of their own exceptionalism comforting and that their aspiring political leaders have been proclaiming it with increasing fervor. Such patriotism has its benefits, but not when it leads to a basic misunderstanding of America's role in the world. This is exactly how bad decisions get made.

America has its own special qualities, as all countries do, but it is still a state embedded in a competitive global system. It is far stronger and richer than most, and its geopolitical position is remarkably favorable. These advantages give the United States a wider range of choice in its conduct of foreign affairs, but they don't ensure that its choices will be good ones. Far from being a unique state whose behavior is radically different from that of other great powers, the United States has behaved like all the rest, pursuing its own self-interest first and foremost, seeking to improve its relative position over time, and devoting relatively little blood or treasure to purely idealistic pursuits. Yet, just like past great powers, it has convinced itself that it is different, and better, than everyone else.

International politics is a contact sport, and even powerful states must compromise their political principles for the sake of security and prosperity. Nationalism is also a powerful force, and it inevitably highlights the country's virtues and sugarcoats its less savory aspects. But if Americans want to be truly exceptional, they might start by viewing the whole idea of "American exceptionalism" with a much more skeptical eye.

The absolute thing this country does not needs to be doing is the exact thing it is doing. Isolating itself, alienating allies, closing its borders. Promoting nationalism on an industrial scale, to the point where white supremists are now empowered to spread their hate openly and without fear of harassment. It is beginning to vaguely remind me of the 1920's when the Ku Klux Klan paraded down the main drag of Washington, D.C. in broad daylight. It's not to the point yet, but it's rapidly approaching that point.

3.

Myth:

The United States Is Responsible for Most of the Good in the World.

Americans are fond of giving themselves credit for positive international developments. President Bill Clinton believed the United States was "indispensable to the forging of stable political relations," and the late Harvard University political scientist Samuel P. Huntington thought U.S. primacy was central "to the future of freedom, democracy, open economies, and international order in the world." Journalist Michael Hirsh has gone even further, writing in his book At War with Ourselves that America's global role is "the greatest gift the world has received in many, many centuries, possibly all of recorded history." Scholarly works such as Tony Smith's America's Mission and G. John Ikenberry's Liberal Leviathan emphasize America's contribution to the spread of democracy and its promotion of a supposedly liberal world order. Given all the high-fives American leaders have given themselves, it is hardly surprising that most Americans see their country as an overwhelmingly positive force in world affairs.

Once again, there is something to this line of argument, just not enough to make it entirely accurate. The United States has made undeniable contributions to peace and stability in the world over the past century, including the Marshall Plan, the creation and management of the Bretton Woods system, its rhetorical support for the core principles of democracy and human rights, and its mostly stabilizing military presence in Europe and the Far East.

But the belief that all good things flow from Washington's wisdom overstates the U.S. contribution by a wide margin.

For starters, though Americans watching Saving Private Ryan or Patton may conclude that the United States played the central role in vanquishing Nazi Germany, most of the fighting was in Eastern Europe and the main burden of defeating Hitler's war machine was borne by the Soviet Union. Similarly, though the Marshall Plan and NATO played important roles in Europe's post-World War II success, Europeans deserve at least as much credit for rebuilding their economies, constructing a novel economic and political union, and moving beyond four centuries of sometimes bitter rivalry. Americans also tend to think they won the Cold War all by themselves, a view that ignores the contributions of other anti-Soviet adversaries and the courageous dissidents whose resistance to communist rule produced the "velvet revolutions" of 1989.

Now, granted if the United States, and it's industrial might had not entered the war when it did, I am quite sure that Germany would have been victorious in World War II. The probability of Germany developing atomic weapons was highly likely and even more likely Germany would have used said atomic weapons is almost a definite. And the United States pretty much fought the Japanese with a little help from the Brits and Aussies by themselves. Now naturally, after the war was over, the United States helped to rebuild not only Europe, but also Japan. Both having suffered severe damage due to allied bombing.

Moreover, as Godfrey Hodgson recently noted in his sympathetic but clear-eyed book, The Myth of American Exceptionalism, the spread of liberal ideals is a global phenomenon with roots in the Enlightenment, and European philosophers and political leaders did much to advance the democratic ideal. Similarly, the abolition of slavery and the long effort to improve the status of women owe more to Britain and other democracies than to the United States, where progress in both areas trailed many other countries.

Nor can the United States claim a global leadership role today on gay rights, criminal justice, or economic equality. Europe's got those areas covered.

Finally, any honest accounting of the past half-century must acknowledge the downside of American primacy. The United States has been the major producer of greenhouse gases for most of the last hundred years and thus a principal cause of the adverse changes that are altering the global environment. The United States stood on the wrong side of the long struggle against apartheid in South Africa and backed plenty of unsavory dictatorships. including Saddam Hussein's, when short-term strategic interests dictated. Americans may be justly proud of their role in creating and defending Israel and in combating global anti-Semitism, but its one-sided policies have also prolonged Palestinian statelessness and sustained Israel's brutal occupation.

Since the 2016 Presidential election and carrying over into the 2020 Presidential election cycle, the rise of domestic terror campaigns brought about by right wing extremists have continued to represent a threat to the very founding principles of our Republic. Groups like the Proud Boys, The Boogaloo Bois, the Wolverine Watchmen and the ever-popular Ku Klux Klan, have not only stepped-up recruiting, but has gotten blessings and support from the President himself. At the absolute least, he has made it acceptable for them to show themselves in public. Earlier in 2020, the FBI, arrested at least 13 of the Wolverine Watchmen militia group, after they allegedly attempted to secure automatic weapons and high explosives to use in an attempt to kidnap and try for treason the Michigan Governor and kill Michigan State Police Officers due to her closure and mask requirement orders. In April or May of 2020, the Governors of Kentucky, Michigan and Wisconsin all saw protestors armed with semi-automatic weapons storm their respective state Capitol buildings in hopes of intimidating the Governor as well as state legislators, who were in session at the time.

I know a lot of this section examines foreign policy, but I say it is the United States' current domestic policies are driving its foreign policy. From deportations, to family separations, to putting children in cages, to unilaterally pulling out of both trade and climate agreements. This "America First" attitude is very dangerous and alienates our allies. Our President cozies up to political strongmen.

Bottom line: Americans take too much credit for global progress and accept too little blame for areas where U.S. policy has in fact been counterproductive. Americans are blind to their weak spots, and in ways that have real-world consequences. Remember when Pentagon planners thought U.S. troops would be greeted in Baghdad with flowers and parades? They mostly got RPGs and IEDs instead.

Marilyn B. Young argues that after the end of the Cold War in 1991, neoconservative intellectuals and policymakers embraced the idea of an "American empire," a national mission to establish freedom and democracy in other nations, particularly poor ones. She argues that after the September 11, 2001 terrorist attacks, the George W. Bush administration reoriented foreign policy to an insistence on maintaining the supreme military and economic power of America, an attitude that harmonized with the new vision of American empire. Young says the Iraq War (2003–2011) exemplified American exceptionalism.

In 2012, the conservative historians Larry Schweikart and Dave Dougherty argued that American exceptionalism be based on four pillars: (1) common law; (2) virtue and morality located in Protestant Christianity; (3) free-market capitalism; and (4) the sanctity of private property.

In a 2015 book, Exceptional: Why the World Needs a Powerful America, former U.S. Vice President Dick Cheney sets out and argues the case for American exceptionalism and concludes: "we are, as Lincoln said, 'the last, best hope of earth.' We are not just one more nation, one more same entity on the world stage. We have been essential to the preservation and progress of freedom, and those who lead us in the years ahead must remind us, as Roosevelt, Kennedy, and Reagan did, of the unique role we play. Neither they nor we should ever forget that we are, in fact, exceptional."

Proponents of American exceptionalism argue that the United States is exceptional in that it was founded on a set of republican ideals rather than on a common heritage, ethnicity, or ruling elite. In the formulation of President Abraham Lincoln in his Gettysburg Address, America is a nation "conceived in liberty, and dedicated to the proposition that all men are created equal." In Lincoln's interpretation, America is inextricably connected with freedom and equality, and the American mission is to ensure "that government of the people, by the people, for the people, shall not perish from the earth." The historian T. Harry Williams argues that Lincoln believed:

In the United States man would create a society that would be the best and the happiest in the world. The United States was the supreme demonstration of democracy. However, the Union did not exist just to make men free in America. It had an even greater mission—to make them free everywhere. By the mere force of its example, America would bring democracy to an undemocratic world.

American policies have been characterized since their inception by a system of federalism (between the states and the federal government) and checks and balances (among the legislative, executive, and judicial branches), which were designed to prevent any faction, region, or government organ from becoming too powerful. Some proponents of the theory of American exceptionalism argue that the system and the accompanying distrust of concentrated power prevent the United States from suffering a "tyranny of the majority," preserve a free republican democracy, and allow citizens to live in a locality whose laws reflect those voters' values. A consequence of the political system is that laws can vary widely across the country. Critics of American exceptionalism maintain that the system merely replaces the power of the federal majority over states with power by the states over local entities. On the balance, the American political system arguably allows for more local dominance but prevents more domestic dominance than a more unitary system would.

It is this idea that we as America has this God given right to impose freedom upon other nations has made it the international bad guy in regards to imposing it's will upon smaller nation states. This has been especially true since the 1970's and the rise of petrol-dollars. We have been simultaneously supplying Israel and its Arab neighbors.

4.

Myth:

America's Success Is Due to Its Special Genius.

The United States has enjoyed remarkable success, and Americans tend to portray their rise to world power as a direct result of the political foresight of the Founding Fathers, the virtues of the U.S. Constitution, the priority placed on individual liberty, and the creativity and hard work of the American people. In this narrative, the United States enjoys an exceptional global position today because it is, well, exceptional.

There is more than a grain of truth to this version of American history. It's not an accident that immigrants came to America in droves in search of economic opportunity, and the "melting pot" myth facilitated the assimilation of each wave of new Americans. America's scientific and technological achievements are fully deserving of praise and owe something to the openness and vitality of the American political order.

The historian Eric Foner has explored the question of birthright citizenship, the provision of the Fourteenth Amendment (1868) that makes anyone born in the United States a full citizen. He argues that: birthright citizenship stands as an example of the much-abused idea of American exceptionalism... birthright citizenship does make the United States (along with Canada) unique in the developed world. No European nation recognizes the principle.

But America's past success is due as much to good luck as to any uniquely American virtues. The new nation was lucky that the continent was lavishly endowed with natural resources and traversed by navigable rivers. It was lucky to have been founded far from the other great powers and even luckier that the native population was less advanced and highly susceptible to European diseases. Americans were fortunate that the European great powers were at war for much of the republic's early history, which greatly facilitated its expansion across the continent, and its global primacy was ensured after the other great powers fought two devastating world wars. This account of America's rise does not deny that the United States did many things right, but it also acknowledges that America's present position owes as much to good fortune as to any special genius or "manifest destiny."

The United States is viewed by many as the great conservative society, but it may also be seen as the most classically liberal polity in the developed world. To understand the exceptional nature of American politics, it is necessary to recognize, with H. G. Wells, that conservatism, as defined outside of the United States, is particularly weak in this country. Conservatism in Europe and Canada, derived from the historic alliance of church and government, is associated with the emergence of the welfare state. The two names most identified with it are Bismarck and Disraeli. Both were leaders of the conservatives (Tories) in their countries. They represented the rural and aristocratic elements, sectors which disdained capitalism, disliked the bourgeoisie, and rejected materialistic values. Their politics reflected the values of noblesse oblige, the obligation of the leaders of society and the economy to protect the less fortunate.

The semantic confusion about liberalism in America arises because both early and latter-day Americans never adopted the term to describe the unique American polity. The reason is simple. The American system of government existed long before the word "liberal" emerged in Napoleonic Spain and was subsequently accepted as referring to a particular party in mid-nineteenth-century England, as distinct from the Tory or Conservative Party. What Europeans have called "liberalism," Americans refer to as "conservatism": a deeply anti-statist doctrine emphasizing the virtues of laissez-faire. Ronald Reagan and Milton Friedman, the two current names most frequently linked with this ideology, define conservatism in America. And as Friedrich Hayek, its most important European exponent noted, it includes the rejection of aristocracy, social class hierarchy, and an established state church. As recently as the April and June 1987 issues of the British magazine Encounter, two leading trans-Atlantic conservative intellectuals, Max Beloff (Lord Beloff) and Irving Kristol, debated the use of titles. Kristol argued that Britain "is soured by a set of very thin, but tenacious, aristocratic pretensions. [which] foreclose opportunities and repress a spirit of equality that has yet to find its full expression." This situation fuels many of the frustrations that make "British life so cheerless, so abounding in ressentiment." Like Tocqueville, he holds up "social equality" as making" other inequalities tolerable in modern democracy." Beloff, a Tory, contended that what threatens conservatism in Britain "is not its remaining links with the aristocratic tradition, but its alleged indifference to some of the abuses of capitalism. It is not the Dukes who lose us votes, but the 'malefactors of great wealth.'" He wondered "why Mr. Kristol believes himself to be a 'conservative,' " since he is "as incapable as most Americans of being a conservative in any profound sense." Lord Beloff concluded that "Conservatism must have a 'Tory' element or it is only the old 'Manchester School,'" i.e., liberal.

Canada's most distinguished conservative intellectual, George Grant, emphasized in his Lament for a Nation that "Americans who call themselves 'Conservatives' have the right to that title only in a particular sense. In fact, they are old-fashioned liberals, their concentration on freedom from governmental interference has more to do with nineteenth century liberalism than with traditional conservatism, which asserts the right of the community to restrain freedom in the name of the common good." Grant bemoaned the fact that American conservatism, with its stress on the virtues of competition and links to business ideology, focuses on the rights of individuals and ignores communal rights and obligations. He noted that there has been no place in the American political philosophy "for the organic conservatism that predates the age of progress. Indeed, the United States is the only society on earth that has no traditions from before the age of progress." The recent efforts, led by Amitai Etzioni, to create a "communitarian" movement are an attempt to transport Toryism to America. British and German Tories have recognized the link and have shown considerable interest in Etzioni's ideas. Still, it must be recognized that American politics have changed. The 1930s produced a qualitative difference. As Richard Hofstadter wrote, this period brought a "social democratic tinge" to the United States for the first time in its history. The Great Depression produced a strong emphasis on planning, on the welfare state, on the role of the government as a major regulatory actor. An earlier upswing in statist sentiment occurred immediately prior to World War 1, as evidenced by the significant support for the largely Republican Progressive movement led by Robert LaFollette and Theodore Roosevelt and the increasing strength (up to a high of 6% of the national vote in 1912) for the Socialist Party. They failed to change the political system. Grant McConnell explains the failure of the Progressive movement as stemming from "the pervasive and latent ambiguity in the movement" about confronting American anti-statist values. "Power as it exists was antagonistic to democracy, but how was it to be curbed without the erection of superior power?"

During the Presidential campaigns which I have witnessed and, thanks to the advent of social media such as Facebook and Twitter, I have been able to be a very vocal supporter of those candidates and a critic of those I did not. During the 2020 Presidential election, there was quite a lot of discussions between my conservative friends and myself. Trust me, I was called a socialist more times than I care to count. I call myself an FDR Progressive, because I advocate for a strong social safety net as well as the taxes in which to pay for it. This immediately puts me at odds with not only my cohorts, but others who do not understand the U.S. Tax Code and the concept of marginal tax rate, which ensures the richest Americans pay an adequate proportional share of taxes relative to their income. I also support not only a strong manufacturing base for our economy, but also collective bargaining for all working Americans. I also support Basic Universal Income as a means of providing a baseline for providing food, clothing and housing for all Americans. Now, do my ideals seem to be a "pie in the sky" vision of our American economic system. Yes, yes it does. Because it gets away from our current system of predatory Capitalism, and back to a gentler approach to Capitalism.

Don't get me wrong, Capitalism sparks and drives innovation. Remember the old saying most of us have heard at one time or another in our lives; "Build a better mousetrap and the world will beat a path to your door." This is definitely a very true statement, look at the progress we have made in just the last century. At the beginning of the 20th Century, the primary sources of transportation were either by railroad or on horseback, now the primary two sources are the automobile and the jet airplane. What used to take months or even weeks to travel from coast to coast not can be achieved in less than 12 hours. But if it not had been for the workers of these companies investing their time, talents and up to and including their lives, progress would not have occurred.

Prior to the 1930s, the American trade union movement was also in its majority anti-statist. The American Federation of Labor (AFL) was syndicalist, believed in more union, not more state power, and was anti-socialist. Its predominant leader for forty years, Samuel Gompers, once said when asked about his politics, that he guessed he was three quarters of an anarchist. And he was right. Europeans and others who perceived the Gompers-led AFL as a conservative organization because it opposed the socialists were wrong. The AFL was an extremely militant organization, which engaged in violence and had a high strike rate. It was not conservative, but rather a militant anti-statist group. The United States also had a revolutionary trade union movement, the Industrial Workers of the World (IWW). The IWW, like the AFL, was not socialist. It was explicitly anarchist, or rather, anarcho-syndicalist. The revived American radical movement of the 1960s, the so-called New Left, was also not socialist. While not doctrinally anarchist, it was much closer to anarchism and the IWW in its ideology and organizational structure than to the Socialists or Communists.

The New Deal, which owed much to the Progressive movement, was not socialist either. Franklin Roosevelt clearly wanted to maintain a capitalist economy. In running for president in 1932, he criticized Herbert Hoover and the Republicans for deficit financing and expanding the economic role of the government, which they had done in order to deal with the Depression. But his New Deal, also rising out of the need to confront the massive economic downsizing, drastically increased the statist strain in American politics, while furthering public support for trade unions. The new labor movement which arose concomitantly, the Committee for (later Congress of) Industrial Organization (CIO), unlike the American Federation of Labor (AFL), was virtually social democratic in its orientation. In fact, socialists and communists played important roles in the movement. The CIO was much more politically active than the older Federation and helped to press the Democrats to the left. The Depression led to a kind of moderate "Europeanization" of American politics, as well as of its labor organizations. Class factors became more important in differentiating party support. The conservatives, increasingly concentrated among the Republicans, remained anti-statist and laissez-faire, but many of them grew willing to accommodate an activist role for the state.

Even at times when foreign companies wanted and even demanded that their plants or facilities where they were located which were Right to Work states, wanted organized labor to be involved in their decision-making processes, the state administrators and politicians resisted for fear it would drive up labor costs and no longer allow them to recruit additional businesses into their respective jurisdictions.

This pattern, however, gradually inverted after World War 11 as a result of long-term prosperity. The United States, like other parts of the developed world, experienced what some have called an economic miracle. The period from 1945 to the 1980s was characterized by considerable growth (mainly before the mid-1970s), an absence of major economic downswings, higher rates of social mobility both on a mass level and into the elites, and a tremendous expansion of higher educational systems--from a few million to 11 or 12 million going to colleges and universities--which fostered that mobility. America did particularly well economically, leading Europe and Japan by a considerable margin in terms of new job creation. A consequence of these developments was a refurbishing of the classical liberal ideology, that is, American conservatism. The class tensions produced by the Depression lessened, reflected in the decline of the labor movement and lower correlations between class position and voting choices. And the members of the small (by comparative standards) American labor movement are today significantly less favorable to government action than European unionists. Fewer than half of American union members are in favor of the government providing a decent standard of living for the unemployed, as compared with 69 percent of West German, 72 percent of British, and 73 percent of Italian unionists. Even before Ronald Reagan entered the White House in 1981, the United States had a lower rate of taxation, a less developed welfare state, and many fewer government-owned industries than other industrialized nations.

The relationship between management and labor in the United States has always been adversarial at best, and violent at its very worst. There has always been a contiguous relationship between management and labor in the United States. This can be traced back to the Puritan work ethic and what is now called Prosperity Gospel or Prosperity Christianity. In a nutshell, this belief is if you lead a respectable and Godly life, God will reward you with material wealth. This has been reemerging as a force within the conservative political thinking for at least the past 20 years, possibly all the way back to the Election of 1980, when Ronald Reagan was elected President and started the age of Mergers and Acquisitions as well as leveraged buyouts where businesses were bought with borrowed money and then carved up and sold piecemeal to not only pay off the debts incurred with the purchase, but huge bonuses for the executives responsible for the purchase. Everyone wins, right? Not even close. Sometimes the companies defaulted on their loans or was forced to file bankruptcy, forcing the company to be sold off at fire sale prices, pension plans were raided, leaving nothing for the workers.

Have we learned or gathered any lessons from the Presidency of Donald J. Trump, possibly the poster boy of the excesses of the 1980's and 90's? I am sad to report, probably not. There are those, particularly right-wing extremists as well as the Religious Right, still believe that Trump was sent by some divine intervention to "Make America Great Again," rescue America from the "Left Wing Socialist Agenda (translated ban abortions, protect the Second Amendment as well as raising taxes,) and keep a level of white supremacy by instilling fear regarding Blacks, Hispanics and Muslims.

Yale Law School Dean Harold Hongju Koh has identified what he says is "the most important respect in which the United States has been genuinely exceptional, about international affairs, international law, and promotion of human rights: namely, in its outstanding global leadership and activism." He argues:

"To this day, the United States remains the only superpower capable, and at times willing, to commit real resources and make real sacrifices to build, sustain, and drive an international system committed to international law, democracy, and the promotion of human rights. Experience teaches that when the United States leads on human rights, from Nuremberg to Kosovo, other countries follow."

Peggy Noonan, an American political pundit, wrote in The Wall Street Journal that "America is not exceptional because it has long attempted to be a force for good in the world, it tries to be a force for good because it is exceptional."

This attitude is exactly where the United States believes it has the God given right to interfere with the internal working of other governments. The most recent being Iraq and Afghanistan, which I might say one of those to needed a regimen change, and it was not Iraq, even though the Bush Administration stated that they had Weapons of Mass Destruction, and they even provided proof, although false, in order to provide justification for invading the country. Now what most people is not aware of is that while Iraq had oil, which the Bush Administration said they could pay for the military actions taken in Iraq. The fly in the ointment was the fact that Iraq told the United States, "No Dice." Now in Afghanistan, the mountains around and in the country having a large amount of rare earth minerals.

Former U.S. Vice President Dick Cheney explores the concept of United States global leadership in a 2015 book on American foreign policy, Exceptional: Why the World Needs a Powerful America, co-authored with his daughter, Liz Cheney, a former official of the U.S. Department of State.

Proponents of American exceptionalism often claim that many features of the "American spirit" were shaped by the frontier process. Following Frederick Jackson Turner's Frontier Thesis, they argue that the American frontier allowed individualism to flourish as pioneers adopted democracy and equality and shed centuries-old European institutions such as royalty, standing armies, established churches, and a landed aristocracy that owned most of the land. However, the frontier experience was not entirely unique to the United States. Other nations had frontiers without them shaping them nearly as much as the American frontier did, usually because they were under the control of a strong national government. South Africa, Russia, Brazil, Argentina, Canada, and Australia had long frontiers, but they did not have "free land" and local control. The political and cultural environments were much different since the other frontiers neither involved widespread ownership of free land nor allowed the settlers to control the local and provincial governments, as was the case in America. Their edge did not shape their national psyches. Each nation had entirely different frontier experiences. For example, the Dutch Boers in South Africa were defeated in war by Britain. In Australia, "mateship" and working together were valued more than individualism was in the United States.

For most of its history, especially from the mid-19th to the early-20th centuries, the United States has been known as the "land of opportunity" and in that sense prided and promoted itself on providing individuals with the opportunity to escape from the contexts of their class and family background. Examples of that social mobility include:

Occupational: children could easily choose careers that were not based upon their parents' choices.

Physical: geographical location was not seen as static, and citizens often relocated freely over long distances without a barrier.

Status: as in most countries, family standing and riches were often a means to remain in a higher social circle. America was notably unusual because if an accepted wisdom that anyone, from poor immigrants upwards, who worked hard could aspire to similar standing, regardless of circumstances of birth. That aspiration is commonly called living the American dream. Birth details were not taken as a social barrier to the upper echelons or high political status in American culture. That stood in contrast to other countries in which many larger offices were socially determined and usually difficult to enter unless one was born into the suitable social group.

However, social mobility in the US is lower than in some European Union countries if it is defined by income movements. American men born into the lowest income quintile are much more likely to stay there than similar people in the Nordic countries or the United Kingdom. Many economists, such as Harvard economist N. Gregory Mankiw, however, state that the discrepancy has little to do with class rigidity; rather, it is a reflection of income disparity: "Moving up and down a short ladder is a lot easier than moving up and down a tall one."

One aspect in America which lends itself to upward social mobility is education, or at least access to education. The veterans of World War II became the first generation to access higher education, thanks to the G.I. Bill. This enabled them to achieve a middle-class income and lifestyle, which allowed their children, the Baby Boomers to go to college en masse. This allowed the American economic engine to flourish. However, the Baby Boomers literally trashed the American manufacturing base in order to satisfy their own greed. It left us with just a service-oriented economy where the majority of Americans barely make enough to make ends meet. In fact, there is no state in these United States where someone can even afford an apartment making minimum wage. Furthermore, the Baby Boomer generation stripped unions of some of their bargaining rights and power, though both destroying companies to enacting Right-to-Work legislation throughout the United States. This has made the worker at best replaceable and at worse expendable, as they have also loosened up workplace regulations. All to feather their nests, but now the Baby Boomers are rapidly retiring, leaving a mess for their child and grandchildren, The Millennials, to try to clean up the mess they made. And I am one from the Baby Boomer generation, so I feel that my critique is valid.

Regarding public welfare, Richard Rose asked in 1989 whether the evidence shows whether the U.S. "is becoming more like other mixed-economy welfare states, or increasingly exceptional." He concluded, "By comparison with other advanced industrial nations America is today exceptional in total public expenditure, in major program priorities, and in the value of public benefits."

Which begs the question to be asked, "Why is the conservative wing of the American political process so hell-bent on doing away with anything that remotely resembles public assistance, Social Security or even Medicare and Medicaid?" Very simply put, they hate these programs because they are successful, but to the purists of the conservative movement, they represent successful governmental programs which just reek of Socialism, and in their view contribute to the largess of government. Grover Norquist, who had at one time had every conservative Congressman and Senator sign a pledge to cut the spending of the Federal government so that it was so small, "He could drown it in a bathtub."

Being a retired social worker, this is something that just grinds my gears. The conservatives wish to cut taxes, yet they are all for a huge defense budget. They are willing to see kids go hungry and Grandma have to choose between medicine or food, just so the Defense Department can have some more toys. While I am in favor of national defense, the question becomes defense against whom? Islamic terrorists? China? Russia? Last time I checked my history, in 1989 the Soviet Union fell because it could not keep up with the defense spending of the United States. In short, we won the Cold War, and then President George H.W. Bush approved closing a large number of US military bases, calling it a "peace dividend."

5.

Myth:

The United States Behaves Better Than Other Nations Do.

Declarations of American exceptionalism rest on the belief that the United States is a uniquely virtuous nation, one that loves peace, nurtures liberty, respects human rights, and embraces the rule of law. Americans like to think their country behaves much better than other states do, and certainly better than other great powers.

If only it were true. The United States may not have been as brutal as the worst states in world history, but a dispassionate look at the historical record belies most claims about America's moral superiority.

Born out of revolution, the United States is a country organized around an ideology which includes a set of dogmas about the nature of a good society. Americanism, as different people have pointed out, is an "ism" or ideology in the same way that communism or fascism or liberalism are isms. As G. K. Chesterton put it: "America is the only nation in the world that is founded on a creed. That creed is set forth with dogmatic and even theological lucidity in the Declaration of Independence." As noted in the Introduction, the nation's ideology can be described in five words: liberty, egalitarianism, individualism, populism, and laissez-faire. The revolutionary ideology which became the American Creed is liberalism in its eighteenth- and nineteenth-century meanings, as distinct from conservative Toryism, statist communitarianism, mercantilism, and noblesse oblige dominant in monarchical, state-church-formed cultures.

Other countries' senses of themselves are derived from a common history. Winston Churchill once gave vivid evidence to the difference between a national identity rooted in history and one defined by ideology in objecting to a proposal in 1940 to outlaw the anti-war Communist Party. In a speech in the House of Commons, Churchill said that as far as he knew, the Communist Party was composed of Englishmen and he did not fear an Englishman. In Europe, nationality is related to community, and thus one cannot become un-English or un-Swedish. Being an American, however, is an ideological commitment. It is not a matter of birth. Those who reject American values are un-American.

This has been a bone of contention of mine is that, beginning in 2016 Presidential election cycle, a definite shift in the winds in regards to political thinking. Ever since the 2010 Congressional election, which saw a purge of moderate Republicans in favor of more radical "Tea Party" Republicans. This was a direct "backlash" against both the policies of then President Barack Obama and also because of the President's ethnic background as well. Never before in the History of the United States was a President judged more on the color of his skin than his accomplishments. Furthermore, Former Secretary of State Hillary Clinton faced off against Donald J. Trump in 2016, Republicans went absolutely insane with Trump's rhetoric regarding illegal immigrants, American manufacturing (or the lack thereof,) government over regulations, the Affordable Care Act, and whether or not President Obama was even a citizen of this country. Of course, once Trump got finished criticizing Obama, he started in on Ms. Clinton beginning with her years as first lady, then as a Senator, finally as Secretary of State. But then again, Trump's complaints about Secretary Clinton was the culmination of thirty years of Republican attacks on her policies and character. And naturally, those who identified as conservative or Evangelical Christian, nodded their heads and actually agreed with their candidate, no matter who he was attacking. And once Trump was in office, he enacted policies which furthered the agenda of the fringe elements of the Republican party. He did so under the guise of "Making America Great Again."

However, what occurred was his embracing of dictatorial strongmen, alienation of our allies, a war of words with Mexico as well as empowering ICE agents to increase their brutality against either people who came to this country, ripping children out of their parent's arms and locking the children in cages before deporting their parents back to where they come from. This was meant to act as a deterrent, approved by the entire cabinet. He also empowered the police to step up their brutality against people of color. The result was the needless deaths of innocent people at the hands of the police, either by gunfire, or being deprived of oxygen via improper restrains.

The United States has been one of the most expansionist powers in modern history. It began as 13 small colonies clinging to the Eastern Seaboard, but eventually expanded across North America, seizing Texas, Arizona, New Mexico, and California from Mexico in 1846. Along the way, it eliminated most of the native population and confined the survivors to impoverished reservations. By the mid-19th century, it had pushed Britain out of the Pacific Northwest and consolidated its hegemony over the Western Hemisphere.

Newspaper reporting the annexation of the Republic of Hawaii in 1898. American exceptionalism has fueled American expansion through the ideology of manifest destiny.

Kammen says that many foreign visitors commented on American exceptionalism including Karl Marx, Francis Lieber, Hermann Eduard von Holst, James Bryce, H. G. Wells, G. K. Chesterton, and Hilaire Belloc and that they did so in complimentary terms. The theme became common, especially in textbooks. From the 1840s to the late 19th century, the McGuffey Readers sold 120 million copies and were studied by most American students. Skrabec (2009) argues the Readers "hailed American exceptionalism, manifest destiny, and America as God's country.... Furthermore, McGuffey saw America as having a future mission to bring liberty and democracy to the world."

The United States has fought numerous wars since then starting several of them and its wartime conduct has hardly been a model of restraint. The 1899-1902 conquest of the Philippines killed some 200,000 to 400,000 Filipinos, most of them civilians, and the United States and its allies did not hesitate to dispatch some 305,000 German and 330,000 Japanese civilians through aerial bombing during World War II, mostly through deliberate campaigns against enemy cities. No wonder Gen. Curtis LeMay, who directed the bombing campaign against Japan, told an aide, "If the U.S. lost the war, we would be prosecuted as war criminals." The United States dropped more than 6 million tons of bombs during the Indochina war, including tons of napalm and lethal defoliants like Agent Orange, and it is directly responsible for the deaths of many of the roughly 1 million civilians who died in that war.

More recently, the U.S.-backed Contra war in Nicaragua killed some 30,000 Nicaraguans, a percentage of their population equivalent to 2 million dead Americans. U.S. military action has led directly or indirectly to the deaths of 250,000 Muslims over the past three decades (and that's a low-end estimate, not counting the deaths resulting from the sanctions against Iraq in the 1990s), including the more than 100,000 people who died following the invasion and occupation of Iraq in 2003. U.S. drones and Special Forces are going after suspected terrorists in at least five countries at present and have killed an unknown number of innocent civilians in the process. Some of these actions may have been necessary to make Americans more prosperous and secure. But while Americans would undoubtedly regard such acts as indefensible if some foreign country were doing them to us, hardly any U.S. politicians have questioned these policies. Instead, Americans still wonder, "Why do they hate us?"

The United States talks a good game on human rights and international law, but it has refused to sign most human rights treaties, is not a party to the International Criminal Court, and has been all too willing to cozy up to dictators remember our friend Hosni Mubarak or The Shah of Iran? — with abysmal human rights records. If that were not enough, the abuses at Abu Ghraib and the George W. Bush administration's reliance on waterboarding, extraordinary rendition, and preventive detention should shake America's belief that it consistently acts in a morally superior fashion. Obama's decision to retain many of these policies suggests they were not a temporary aberration.

The United States never conquered a vast overseas empire or caused millions to die through tyrannical blunders like China's Great Leap Forward or Stalin's forced collectivization. And given the vast power at its disposal for much of the past century, Washington could certainly have done much worse. But the record is clear: U.S. leaders have done what they thought they had to do when confronted by external dangers, and they paid scant attention to moral principles along the way. The idea that the United States is uniquely virtuous may be comforting to Americans; too bad it's not true.

Many scholars use a model of American exceptionalism developed by Harvard political scientist Louis Hartz. In the Liberal Tradition in America (1955), Hartz argued that the American political tradition lacks the left-wing/socialist and right-wing/aristocratic elements that dominated in most other lands because colonial America lacked feudal traditions, such as established churches, landed estates, and a hereditary nobility, although some European practices of feudal origin, such as primogeniture and indentured service, were transmitted to America. The "liberal consensus" school, typified by David Potter, Daniel Boorstin, and Richard Hofstadter followed Hartz in emphasizing that political conflicts in American history remained within the tight boundaries of a liberal consensus regarding private property, individual rights, and representative government. The national government that emerged was far less centralized or nationalized than its European counterparts.

The American Revolution sharply weakened the noblesse oblige, hierarchically rooted, organic community values which had been linked to Tory sentiments, and enormously strengthened the individualistic, egalitarian, and anti-statist ones which had been present in the settler and religious background of the colonies. These values were evident in the twentieth-century fact that, as H. G. Wells pointed out close to ninety years ago, the United States not only has lacked a viable socialist party, but also has never developed a British or European-type Conservative or Tory party. Rather, America has been dominated by pure bourgeois, middle-class individualistic values. As Wells put it: "Essentially America is a middle-class [which has] become a community and so its essential problems are the problems of a modern individualistic society, stark and clear." He enunciated a theory of America as a liberal society, in the classic anti-statist meaning of the term:

It is not difficult to show for example, that the two great political parties in America represent only one English party, the middle-class Liberal party. There are no Tories, and no Labor Party. The new world was left to the Whigs and Nonconformists and to those less constructive, less logical, more popular and liberating thinkers who became Radicals in England, and Jeffersonians and then Democrats in America. All Americans are, from the English point of view, Liberals of one sort or another. The liberalism of the eighteenth century was essentially the rebellion, against the monarchical and aristocratic state against hereditary privilege, against restrictions on bargains. Its spirit was essentially anarchistic--the antithesis of Socialism. It was anti-State.

The notion of "American exceptionalism" became widely applied in the context of efforts to account for the weakness of working-class radicalism in the United States. The major question subsumed in the concept became why the United States is the only industrialized country which does not have a significant socialist movement or Labor party. That riddle has bedeviled socialist theorists since the late nineteenth century. Friedrich Engels tried to answer it in the last decade of his life. The German socialist and sociologist Werner Sombart dealt with it in a major book published in his native language in 1906, Why Is There No Socialism in the United States? As we have seen, H. G. Wells, then a Fabian, also addressed the issue that year in The Future in America. Both Lenin and Trotsky were deeply concerned because the logic of Marxism, the proposition expressed by Marx in Das Kapital that "the more developed country shows the less developed the image of their future," implied to Marxists prior to the Russian Revolution that the United States would be the first socialist country."

That is why the Republican party is so adamantly opposed to any kind of social assistance program. They feel that any type of assistance is viewed as socialistic and a deterrent to them being a productive member of the society. This includes the disabled, the very old and very young. The government should not be in the business of providing healthcare, pensions or food, Yet the programs of both Medicare and Medicaid, Social Security and Disability benefits, as well as the Supplemental Nutritional Assistance Program all prove beneficial for our economy. From giving monies to people to spend, to providing farmers a market for their produce, even these programs prove beneficial to others beyond their intended recipients.

Since some object to an attempt to explain a negative, a vacancy, the query may of course be reversed to ask why has America been the most classically liberal polity in the world from its founding to the present? Although the United States remains the wealthiest large industrialized nation, it devotes less of its income to welfare and the state is less involved in the economy than is true for other developed countries. It not only does not have a viable, class-conscious, radical political movement, but its trade unions, which have long been weaker than those of almost all other industrialized countries, have been steadily declining since the mid-1950s. An emphasis on American uniqueness raises the obvious question of the nature of the differences. There is a large literature dating back to at least the eighteenth century which attempts to specify the special character of the United States politically and socially. One of the most interesting, often overlooked, is Edmund Burke's speech to the House of Commons proposing reconciliation with the colonies, in which he sought to explain to his fellow members what the revolutionary Americans were like. He noted that they were different culturally, that they were not simply transplanted Englishmen. He particularly stressed the unique character of American religion. J. Hector St. John Crevecoeur, in his book Letters from an American Farmer, written in the late eighteenth century, explicitly raised the question, "What is an American?" He emphasized that Americans behaved differently in their social relations, were much more egalitarian than other nationalities, that their "dictionary" was "short in words of dignity, and names of honor," that is, in terms through which the lower strata expressed their subservience to the higher. Tocqueville, who observed egalitarianism in a similar fashion, also stressed individualism, as distinct from the emphasis on "group ties" which marked Europe.

These commentaries have been followed by a myriad--thousands upon thousands--of books and articles by foreign travelers. The overwhelming majority are by educated Europeans. Such writings are fruitful because they are comparative; those who wrote them emphasized cross-national variations in behavior and institutions. Tocqueville's Democracy, of course, is the best known. As we have seen, he noted that he never wrote anything about the United States without thinking of France. As he put it, in speaking of his need to contrast the same institutions and behavior in both countries, "without comparisons to make, the mind doesn't know how to proceed." Harriet Martineau, an English contemporary, also wrote a first-rate comparative book on America. Friedrich Engels and Max Weber were among the contributors to the literature. There is a fairly systematic and similar logic in many of these discussions. Beyond the analysis of variations between the United States and Europe, various other comparisons have been fruitful. In previous writings, I have suggested that one of the best ways to specify and distinguish American traits is by contrast with Canada. There is a considerable comparative North American literature, written almost entirely by Canadians. They have a great advantage over Americans since, while very few of the latter study their northern neighbor, it is impossible to be a literate Canadian without knowing almost as much, if not more, as most Americans about the United States. Almost every Canadian work on a given subject (the city, religion, the family, trade unions, etc.) contains a great deal about the United States. Many Canadians seek to explain their own country by dealing with differences or similarities south of the border. Specifying and analyzing variations among the predominantly English-speaking countries--Australia, Canada, Great Britain, New Zealand, and the United States--is also useful precisely because the differences among them generally are smaller than between each and non-Anglophonic societies. have tried to analyze these variations in The First New Nation. The logic of studying societies which have major aspects in common was also followed by Louis Hartz in treating the overseas settler societies--United States, Canada, Latin America, Australia, and South Africa--as units for comparison. Fruitful comparisons have been made between Latin America and Anglophonic North America, which shed light on each.

Some Latin Americans have argued that there are major common elements in the Americas which show up in comparisons with Europe. Fernando Cardoso, a distinguished sociologist and now president of Brazil, once told me that he and his friends (who were activists in the underground left in the early 1960s) consciously decided not to found a socialist party as the military dictatorship was breaking down. They formed a populist party because, as they read the evidence, class-conscious socialism does not appeal in the Americas. With the exceptions of Chile and Canada (to a limited extent), major New World left parties from Argentina to the United States have been populist. Cardoso suggested that consciousness of social class is less salient throughout most of the Americas than in post-feudal Europe. However, I do not want to take on the issue of how exceptional the Americas are; dealing with the United States is more than enough.

7.

Myth:

There Is Something Exceptional About American Exceptional-ism.

Whenever American leaders refer to the "unique" responsibilities of the United States, they are saying that it is different from other powers and that these differences require them to take on special burdens.

Yet there is nothing unusual about such lofty declarations; indeed, those who make them are treading a well-worn path. Most great powers have considered themselves superior to their rivals and have believed that they were advancing some greater good when they imposed their preferences on others. The British thought they were bearing the "white man's burden," while French colonialists invoked la mission civilisatrice to justify their empire. Portugal, whose imperial activities were hardly distinguished, believed it was promoting a certain missão civilizadora. Even many of the officials of the former Soviet Union genuinely believed they were leading the world toward a socialist utopia despite the many cruelties that communist rule inflicted. Of course, the United States has by far the better claim to virtue than Stalin or his successors, but Obama was right to remind us that all countries prize their own particular qualities.

When Americans proclaim, they are exceptional and indispensable, they are simply the latest nation to sing a familiar old song. Among great powers, thinking you're special is the norm, not the exception.

Every time a public figure uses the term "American exceptionalism," ordinary Americans will stand up, cheer and agree, usually have little to no idea what they think is exceptional about America, other than what they have been programmed to believe it means. It's number one for a quick answer to the question: "What is American exceptionalism?" The latest benefactor was Hillary Clinton, who used the term in a speech on 31 August. Until about 2010, few Americans had heard the term. Since then, its use has expanded exponentially. It is strange that such an inelegant term should be adopted by two major political parties when so many people had not a clue what it meant. Of course, one doesn't have to use the term to believe in the underlying concept. But the phrase has a history that helps us to understand the current hyperbolic use.

American exceptionalism is not the same as saying the United States is "different" from other countries. It doesn't just mean that the U.S. is "unique." Countries, like people, are all different and unique, even if many share some underlying characteristics. Exceptionalism requires something far more: a belief that the U.S. follows a path of history different from the laws or norms that govern other countries. That's the essence of American exceptionalism: The U.S. is not just a bigger and more powerful country — but an exception. It is the bearer of freedom and liberty, and morally superior to something called "Europe." Never mind the differences within Europe, or the fact that "the world" is bigger than the U.S. and Europe. The "Europe" versus "America" dichotomy is the crucible in which American exceptionalist thinking formed.

Some presume that the Frenchman Alexis de Tocqueville invented the term in the 1830s, but only once did de Tocqueville actually call American society "exceptional." He argued that Americans lacked culture and science, but could rely on the Anglo-Saxons in Britain to supply the higher forms of civilization. This is not what Americans mean by "exceptionalism" today.

American exceptionalism is an ideology. The "ism" is the give-away. De Tocqueville examined U.S. institutions and moral behaviors as structural tendencies of democratic societies. He did not see U.S. democracy as an ideology. To him, the U.S. was the harbinger of a future that involved the possible democratization of Europe, not an unrepeatable outlier of civilization. He studied the U.S. as a model of democratic society, whose workings needed to be understood, because the idea was spreading.

Some think that Werner Sombart, the German socialist of the early 1900s, invented the term, but he did not. Sombart claimed only that U.S. capitalism, and its abundance, made the country temporarily unfavorable terrain for the development of socialism. It was actually Joseph Stalin, or his minions, who, in 1929, gave the idea its name. It is surely one of the ironies of modern history that both major U.S. political parties now compete to endorse a Stalinist term.

Orthodox communists used the term to condemn the heretical views of the American communist Jay Lovestone. In the late 1920s, Lovestone argued that the capitalist economy of the U.S. did not promote the revolutionary moment for which all communists waited. The Communist Party expelled Lovestone, but his followers and ex-Trotskyites in the U.S. embraced the exceptionalist epithet and, eventually, the idea that the U.S. would permanently avoid the socialist stage of development.

After the Nazi-Soviet Pact of 1941, as well as later during the Cold War, many of these U.S. Marxists jettisoned their old political allegiances but retained the mindset that the economic success of the U.S. buried class struggle in their nation — permanently. As the leader of the free world, the chief victor in the Second World War over "totalitarian" Germany, and by far the world's most prosperous economy, the U.S. seemed in all these ways an exceptional nation. Seymour Martin Lipset, the eminent Stanford political sociologist, made a career investigating the many factors that led to this American exceptionalism. Until his death in 2006, Lipset continued to hold that the U.S. was not subject to the historical norms of all other nations.

No one did more than Ronald Reagan to amplify and popularize the U.S. as exceptional. Refusing to accept the doldrums of the Jimmy Carter presidency or the transgressions of Richard Nixon as the best that Americans could do, Reagan promoted the image of the U.S. as a shining "city upon a hill." This reference is to a 1630 sermon by John Winthrop, the Governor of Massachusetts Bay Colony. Winthrop was calling on the new Pilgrim settlers heading for Massachusetts to stick to the narrow path of Puritanism.

Reagan and his followers wrongly attributed American exceptionalism to this Puritan injunction, and added "shining" to the original, which gave the phrase a distinctly different connotation. Nor was Winthrop referring to any nation, but rather a discrete community of English Protestant believers. Notably, Winthrop's sermon had been neglected for centuries. It was resurrected only in the 1940s by a few Harvard academics who were engaged in an intellectual rehabilitation of Puritan thought. In a 1961 speech, John F. Kennedy, who had been a Harvard student and was influenced by that university's Americanists, used the "city upon a hill" phrase. The idea of the U.S. as a "city upon a hill," however, really gained purchase in political rhetoric in the 1970s and '80s, as Reagan sought to reinvent the country.

Without question, Reagan saw the U.S. as an exceptional nation. The language of exceptionalism, however, derived from Marxism, not God. The idea of a morally superior and unique civilization destined to guide the world did not come under the banner of an orthodox "ism" until very recently, until the 21st century. In the wake of 9/11, the speeches of George W. Bush and his supporters asserted the radical distinctiveness of the U.S. with a new belligerence. We have all heard it: It is "our freedoms" that Islamic terrorists hated; they wished to kill Americans because they envied this exceptional inheritance.

The global financial crisis of 2007-10 added to the geopolitical turmoil that followed 9/11. Though the U.S. economy expanded in the 1990s and early 2000s, economic inequality that began to grow in the Reagan era also became worse. In the post-1945 age, when academics first posed American exceptionalism as a coherent doctrine, the idea also became linked to global U.S. military and political hegemony. In the past two generations, since the Reagan era, Americans have not prospered to the same extent, and American exceptionalism has been increasingly linked only to military hegemony. As evidenced by an increase in military spending, to the point where we spent more than the next 29 other countries, 28 of whom are our allies.

Decline is, in fact, the midwife to the ideology of American exceptionalism. The less exceptional that circumstances in the U.S. appear, the louder defenders of exceptionalism insist on orthodoxy. When the nation was indisputably powerful and its people prosperous, Americans did not collectively require an "ism" to serve as a guiding light. In these more polarized times, when the fates of Americans become based more on their class and less on their shared nationality, the ideological orthodoxy of American exceptionalism has emerged on a political level. A previously obscure academic term became a rallying cry for a political agenda.

When Hillary Clinton, in 2016, joined the exceptionalist bandwagon, it reflects a political consensus that Donald Trump denies. In wanting to make America great again, Trump implicitly accepts that it is not currently "great," and never was exceptional. No longer is the Republican Party the chief cheerleader of American exceptionalism. But the Democrats have picked up the mantle, and the language of exceptionalism continues to rally a party and a country.

So now the question begs to be asked, what was the purpose of Trump using the two quotes, "Make America Great Again," and "Keep America Great," as his campaign slogans? Very simple, Trump being a businessman, understands the value of marketing and branding. He used a phrase which would tap into American's patriotism and a longing to return to the good ol' days. You know, the ones the Republican party always preaches. A return to the family values of the 1950's. the economic policies of the 1920's, and the labor practices of the 1890's. My opinion is, and this is a cynical one, that Trump used these two phrases in order to tap into the desperation of the American people who have seen the Middle class of this country shrink, the rise of the working poor, the rise of the cost of a college education, which has saddled several college graduates with insurmountable debt. This has generated a considerable amount of anxiety amongst voters, especially white Americans, who see the progressive direction in this country eroding their positions of privilege. They believe that minorities are taking away their jobs, and getting special breaks that they should only be entitled. They do not like having to press, "One," for English. And if anyone who has read anything about the future of America knows the white race in the United States will be a minority race within the next 15 to 20 years.

These are just a few examples of white anxiety in this country, the one thing that conservatives cling to, white fear and angry old white men, they keep hounding the minorities are the root cause of all the woes in this country. They ignore the normal ebbs and flows of a Capitalist economy, preferring rather to focus upon tapping into unreasonable beliefs and long held prejudices of the masses.

My question is "When was America ever great?" That is a question we shall explore further in an upcoming chapter.

6.

We allowed an important idea, American exceptionalism, to be hijacked and misused. Now we need to rescue that idea and let it guide America at home and abroad. Can America still lead the world? Should it? If so, how? These fundamental questions have lurked in the background for years. Donald Trump brought them front and center.

The knee-jerk response of national-security professionals to such questions is to offer a history lesson on the benefits of the "liberal international order" that America built after 1945. Folks of my age and era were treated to the philosophy the America was the Greatest nation on the face of the Earth, without exception. That many men died for us to have the privilege of being an American. Young people have been exposed to a particularly arrogant brand of exceptionalism. Times have changed. Young people have had a profoundly different upbringing. They were in elementary and middle school in the 2000s, children of the global War on Terror —of Guantánamo and Abu Ghraib, drones and Edward Snowden, and, most of all, the Iraq War. Many of them aren't naturally inclined to see American foreign policy through a lens of optimism or aspiration. I see it in surveys that reveal a strong generational divide over the idea of "American exceptionalism." Large numbers of young people question the merits of a unique American leadership role in world affairs.

This is partly because they have seen the country's foreign policy so frequently fall short. But I suspect it is also because they have been exposed to a particularly arrogant brand of exceptionalism. For example, Dick Cheney and his daughter Liz published a book a few years ago called Exceptional, in which they boast of America's unmatched "goodness" and "greatness"—conceding nothing, admitting no error. In their telling, the Vietnam and Iraq Wars were sound strategic decisions. George W. Bush's administration's use of torture was right; its critics were wrong. And on and on. Young people hear these kinds of arguments and say, Count us out.

Meanwhile, older generations are tilting toward a different outlook: The United States as the world's No. 1 sucker. It's time, many believe, to stop shouldering the burdens and letting others enjoy the benefits. This is Trump's vision of "America first." He is hostile toward America's allies and contemptuous of cooperation. He loves to goad and bully (and even bomb) other countries and says alarming and irresponsible things about nuclear war. He has pulled out of the Iran nuclear deal, the Paris climate agreement, the Trans-Pacific Partnership, and more. He is not preaching isolationism; he is preaching predatory unilateralism. Now these older generations include my own; The Baby Boomers. You remember them, don't you? They were also the long haired, pot smoking hippies of the 1960's who protested the Vietnam conflict and called those who did serve as "baby killers," causing a divide in this country which took about 20 years to heal. Then during the 1970's, they wore leisure suits, danced to Disco music, had literally a ton of sex, and helped bring about the AIDS crisis in this country. Then sometime between the 1970's and 1980, they got a haircut, put on Khaki's and started working in Corporate America, supporting a lot of the corporate raids as well as the mergers and acquisitions. This made a few stinking wealthy, while for the majority did not fare so well. Lay-offs, retraining, having to relocate, loss of union representation, loss of health and welfare benefits, and finally the loss of their pensions. All thanks to the greed of one selfish, entitled generation.

Trump's approach is dangerous, but he has surfaced questions that need clear answers. Those of us who believe that the United States can and should continue to occupy a global leadership role, even if a different role than in the past, have to explain why Trump is wrong—and provide a better strategy for the future.

In doing so, we should not play by his rules. An energized, inspiring, and ultimately successful foreign policy must cut through Trump's false, dog-whistling choice between globalism and nationalism. It must combine the best kind of patriotism (a shared civic spirit and a clear sense of the national interest) and the best kind of internationalism (a recognition that when your neighbor's house is on fire, you need to grab a bucket). And it should reject the worst kind of nationalism (damn-the-consequences aggression and identity-based hate-mongering) and the worst kind of internationalism (the self-congratulatory insulation of the Davos elite).

Of course, Trump's style of nationalism played right into the hands of white supremists and nationalists. These folks have a limited grasp of being part of the global economy or anything that might suggest that others (particularly those of certain races,) may be smarter, better educated, or more talented than they are. This slaps directly in the face of Caucasian superiority. That is why Trump, during the 2020 campaign, kept trying to elicit fear among white suburban housewives that certain minorities were coming to the suburbs, bringing with them lower property values, higher crime, drugs and violence. This argument was straight out of the Jim Crow playbook of the 1950's, an idea I was even taught in elementary school in the 1970's. Goes to show you that prejudice is a learned behavior. Of course, this makes for fertile ground for fascism to take root and thrive in this country.

This calls for rescuing the idea of American exceptionalism from both its chest-thumping proponents and its cynical critics, and renewing it for the present time. The idea is not that the United States is intrinsically better than other countries, but rather this: Despite its flaws, America possesses distinctive attributes that can be put to work to advance both the national interest and the larger common interest.

In the wrong hands, American exceptionalism can be a dangerous idea. It can justify too much. It can admit too little. It can offend and alienate. But for proponents of an engaged and effective foreign policy, failure to own and define the idea—especially when malevolent forces are seeking to own and define so many national ideas—is even more dangerous. Without a sense of greater purpose about the nation's work in the world, the U.S. will lose direction and ambition at a time when it badly needs both. And if that sense of purpose is not grounded in humility, the U.S. will fall victim to hubris and excess.

What follows is a case for a new American exceptionalism as the answer to Donald Trump's "America first"—and as the basis for American leadership in the 21st century.

American exceptionalism has meant different things to different people at different times: the unique geographic advantages of the continent, the story of the Revolution and the writing of the Constitution, the legacy of the frontier, the impulse to universalize the American experience. Some have taken this to an extreme, asserting that America is blessed by divine providence.

There is a common thread: the idea that the United States has a set of characteristics that gives it a unique capacity and responsibility to help make the world a better place.

Most people are familiar with the standard story of how those characteristics have guided American foreign policy in the modern era. The United States stopped Hitler's Germany, saved Western Europe from economic ruin, stood firm against the Soviet Union, and supported the spread of democracy worldwide. This story has always been compelling. It is also incomplete. Americans are no longer buying it at face value. What about the mistakes, the complexities, the imperfections—things like covert regime change across Latin America, support for brutal dictators, the invasion of Iraq, and the tragedies (despite the best of intentions) of Somalia and Libya? The Cheney version either ignores this dark underbelly or insists that the United States is "saved," as it were, and therefore cannot sin. It is a self-serving lie that has generated skepticism about America's strengths and virtues.

Still, the exceptionalist idea has proved resilient, no matter how many experts declare it useless or wrong. The expectation that the United States can do, and be, better runs deep—even among America's fiercest critics. One such critic, the journalist Suzy Hansen, used the phrase broken heart in her book, "Notes on a Foreign Country," to describe the way many people feel about the reality of American power. The phrase reflects a perhaps unwitting expectation, a hope, that the U.S. will act differently from other powerful countries. The idea of American exceptionalism speaks to not just who we have been but who we can be.

A distinctive part of America's postwar history has been the ability to adjust after failures and follies, which are an inevitable part of global leadership. The Marshall Plan and NATO came into being only after a period in which Harry Truman's administration reduced the American footprint in Western Europe and imposed self-defeating conditions on economic assistance. The Bush-era HIV/aids program that saved millions of lives arrived many years after the woeful response to the epidemic by Ronald Reagan's administration. In Latin America, from the end of the Cold War through the Barack Obama years, heavy-handed intervention and support for dictators gave way to mutual respect, engagement as equals, and the normalization of relations with Cuba.

This capacity for self-appraisal, self-correction, and self-renewal separates the United States from past superpowers. It is what President Obama, elected in part because of popular opposition to the Iraq War, meant when he said, on the 50th anniversary of the march to Montgomery, Alabama: "Each successive generation can look upon our imperfections and decide that it is in our power to remake this nation to more closely align with our highest ideals."

Just as the election of Donald Trump was both a backlash against Barack Obama, being the first Black President, and Hillary Clinton, who could have been the nation's first female President. Trump used a tried-and-true method among Republicans, stoking fear among the electorate. But instead of using veiled language, Trump went ahead and spoke what was normally spoken of in hushed tones. He called those coming over the southern border, "murderers and rapists," called out all Muslims as "Terrorists." This drove the crowds into an almost absolute frenzy, especially if those Trump was discussing happened to be of a darker skin tone. The appealed to the absolute worst of American values, namely racism, xenophobia, and a belief in the superiority of the Caucasian race.

After Trump, the United States will face its next great readjustment. Part of the challenge will be to repair the damage he has done—to alliances, to treaties, to the perception of American motives, to trust in America's word, and, most of all, to the very idea of America. But the United States must also update its purpose in a changing world.

In the immediate aftermath of the Second World War, U.S. foreign policy was rooted in a single, simple idea: Americans were not willing to endure global war and global depression ever again. The Cold War followed quickly, and provided a clarity of purpose to efforts both at home and overseas. When the Soviet Union collapsed, so did the guiding objectives of U.S. foreign policy. Exceptionalism began to mean, in the words of the political scientist Stanley Hoffmann, nothing more than "being, remaining, and acting as the only superpower." Then came 9/11. America stumbled into the War on Terror, which started with the justified invasion of Afghanistan but continued with the invasion of Iraq, one of the most catastrophic decisions in American history. The result, a decade and a half later, is an open-ended military commitment that spans multiple countries.

Today, three decades after the fall of the Berlin Wall, the U.S. still hasn't found a durable answer to the most basic of questions: What is American foreign policy for?

The foreign-policy community's traditional response to that question has been to describe America as the world's "indispensable nation." That is no longer sufficient. By itself, indispensability is more wearying than energizing—it's the boy in the Hans Brinker story, holding back the flood by putting his finger in the dike. It speaks to fulfilling others' needs, not one's own. And it comes with no limits. That is why Trump's "America First" doesn't work and will never work in the 21st Century, countries are now too interdependent upon each other.

The core purpose of American foreign policy must be to protect and defend the American way of life. This raises the obvious challenge that the very definition of the American way of life is currently up for grabs. No vision of American exceptionalism can succeed if the United States does not defeat the emerging vision that emphasizes ethnic and cultural identity and restore a more hopeful and inclusive definition: a healthy democracy, shared economic prosperity, and security and freedom for all citizens to follow the paths they choose. This requires domestic renewal above all, with energetic responses at home to the rise of tribalism and the hollowing-out of the middle class. Foreign policy can support that renewal, while dealing effectively with external threats.

These fall into two categories. The first emanate from other countries, specifically the major powers: There is China's long-term strategy to dominate the fastest-growing part of the world, to make the global economy adjust to its brand of authoritarian capitalism, and above all to put pressure on free and open economic and political models. And there is Russia's pursuit of a related strategy to spread neofascist ideology and destabilize Western democracies. The threats in the second category are those that transcend national borders: the spread of weapons of mass destruction; deadly epidemics like Ebola; irreversible planetary harm caused by climate change; another global economic melt-down; and massive cyberattacks.

All of these have the potential to cripple America as we know it. Here's the kicker: None of them can be effectively confronted by the United States alone, and none can be effectively confronted if the United States sits on the sidelines.

The fact that the major powers have not returned to war with one another since 1945 is a remarkable achievement of American statecraft.

The U.S. must mobilize a common response to these threats. In some cases, the response needs to be global, bringing the U.S. together with its rivals—including China—to face shared challenges such as nuclear proliferation and climate change. In others, the U.S. should work exclusively with its friends and allies to resist the spread of aggression, authoritarianism, and malignant corruption.

Cooperation of this kind does not happen spontaneously; it requires some actor to step up and lead. The U.S. has historically served this function, a reality I experienced firsthand during my time in government. If the U.S. had not led the charge, the Paris Agreement—which rallied 195 nations to pledge to reduce carbon emissions—would not have come into being. If, after a sluggish start, the U.S. had not led the response to the Ebola outbreak in 2014, an epidemic could have swept across Africa and proved difficult to contain. And even when the U.S. makes mistakes at home, its leadership abroad can come to the rescue: If the U.S. had not coordinated a global response, the 2008 financial crisis could easily have spiraled into a second Great Depression.

Consider what would happen if America gave up its leadership role. Might China fill the gap? I have not seen anyone make a persuasive case that China would or could, and in any event, China sometimes is the threat. The Europeans cannot replace America either, given how preoccupied they are with holding their own union together. However, Chancellor Merkel of Germany did step up while Trump was speaking so highly of Vladimir Putin, President Xi of China, and other strongmen around the planet, to be at least temporary, as the leader of the free world.

While the Trump administration's belief in an "America First" policy has led us to become more isolated from the rest of the world's stage, this is not something new. Just in the twentieth century, America attempted twice to take an isolated stance in regards to the affairs of other countries. The first was in the years prior to World War I, where even President Woodrow Wilson did not want the United States involved in what most Americans believed was a European matter. However, after the torpedoing of several ocean liners by German U-Boats, Wilson had little choice but to ask Congress for a declaration of war.

After winning World War I, Wilson, ever the pragmatic optimist, helped create what would be called The League of Nations. His rationale was simple, since the United States helped "make the world safe for Democracy," he believed that it was rational to have an organization to prevent war. Except three things occurred which set the world up for World War II. First, Wilson had a stroke in 1919, leaving him confined to his bed and unable to lobby the Senate to approve the Treaty of Versailles. Second, the victorious side of the war in Europe wanted to punish Germany, by taking away their Army and Navy, as well as making them pay huge reparations to the allied powers. And third and finally, the American people were tired of the war and wanted to look inward and enjoy the peace and prosperity they had earned. They left their elected Senators know this, and the Senate did not ratify The Treaty of Versailles, they did ratify another peace treaty with the Central powers later though.

Naturally, in the years leading up to World War II, it was also American sentiment that it was again a European conflict and the United States had no business intervening. However, the United States did have a Lend/Lease program with the United Kingdom in order to provide materials for them to wage war against the Axis powers, namely Germany and Italy. Japan was still busy in Asia attempting to expand their Empire. However, all this changed on December 7, 1941, when the Japanese attacked the U.S. Naval Base at Pearl Harbor, Hawaii. President Roosevelt sought a declaration of war against Japan on December 8, 1941, which was approved later that day. Germany and Italy declared war on the United States on December 10, 1941. After four long, hard years of fighting, Germany surrendered in May, 1945, while Italy overthrew Mussolini in 1944 and he was summarily executed. Japan finally formally surrendered in September, 1945 after two atomic bombs decimated to cities of Hiroshima and Nagasaki.

After World War II, a massive rebuilding effort led by the United States for both Europe and Japan. As a result, countries in Europe as well as Japan, turned out to become economic powerhouses which dominated the United States during the 1980's. It wasn't until an economic contraction in the early 1990's caused Japan to realize it had overextended itself financially and had to massively scale back its worldwide presence that this slowed down Japan's economic engine. While Europe experience similar contraction, but due to them, primarily the German's being more conservative with their growth, they weathered the contraction better than their Japanese counterparts.

How does exceptionalism fit into this analysis? The United States cannot keep leading if it starts being seen by others as a "normal" power, interested exclusively in its narrow self-interest. America has to keep demonstrating that it is an unusual power, in terms of its attitudes, habits, methods, and ideas. Being exceptional means putting these core attributes to work for America's own interests, yes—but also for the common good. Similarly, at home, the public will accept major investment in foreign policy only if it believes the United States is not just a normal country, with normal responsibilities. Exceptionalism is how you reconcile patriotism with internationalism. For instance, the recent COVID-19 pandemic shed light on two major flaws in our American system. First, was a lack of Universal Health Care coverage, as evidenced by when all the workers (an estimated 22 million of them,) lost their jobs also lost their health care. Trust me, having no health insurance during a pandemic is not a position one would like to find themselves. Second, was a lack of basic income to provide for food, clothing and shelter. Universal Basic Income is a relatively new concept which has appeared to address those working minimum and sub-minimum wage (such as the food industry and hospitality) workers, to cover their basic needs, no more, no less. Will taxes have to be raised? Yes. But will those taxes benefit those who need it the most? Definitely. But it will take leadership and bipartisan cooperation, something almost unheard of in our respective state and national capitols these days.

A national idea like American exceptionalism will fail, however, if it is neither plausible nor well defined. We should therefore identify the distinctive attributes of the United States, explain how to revive and reinforce them, and prescribe how to put them to work in foreign policy.

The first of those attributes has been a recognition that the best and most durable solutions are ones in which America's gain also contributes to gains by others. From the republican ideas of the Founders—in particular, from their notion of interdependence— flows an attitude. Alexis de Tocqueville called it "self-interest rightly understood." Today, we might call it positive-sum thinking.

This attitude guided America's grand strategy after the Second World War, as the U.S. rebuilt vanquished foes, protected the sea lanes, and responded to natural disasters halfway around the world. For centuries, European states waged war with grim regularity. The fact that the major powers have not returned to war with one another since 1945 is a remarkable achievement of

American statecraft. Meanwhile, China's extraordinary development was the result not of failures in U.S. foreign policy but of its successes. The U.S. maintained the security that helped drive remarkable economic growth across the Asia-Pacific region.

This is why so many observers around the world fear American retreat more than they fear American domination. During my time in the Obama administration, when I talked with counterparts in the Middle East or East Asia, I often heard a litany of complaints about things the United States had done, punctuated by a demand that the United States do more. It reminded me of the classic restaurant joke: "The food here is terrible, and such small portions!"

At some level, most of the world knows that America's positive-sum approach is valuable and unusual. At a gathering of Asian nations in 2011, I heard the Chinese foreign minister address the issue of Beijing's ambitions in the South China Sea this way: "China is a big country, and other countries here are small countries. Think hard about that." This is China's way, and Russia's way. It generally has not been America's way.

That is, it wasn't until Trump came along. He treats foreign policy in simple terms: us against them. He sizes up the European Union and NATO and sees a bunch of smaller countries banding together to take advantage of the United States, on trade, security, migration, you name it. Trump's worldview is one of grievance and victimization: "They're laughing at us." The U.S. must reject the mafia logic, "Pay up or else," that Trump has applied to America's alliances. The country's allies are a special national asset. The U.S. can rely on dozens of strong, independent nations to help thwart terror attacks, resist aggression by adversaries, and more, in a way no rival can. China's spending spree around the world has failed to buy it a single reliable ally.

While Trump was correct in his assessment that the rest of the world was laughing at us, he failed to see who they were actually were laughing at, namely him. He was this overgrown man-child attempting to hang with people who had been in government for years or even decades, as a businessman, he lacked the savvy and finesse of diplomacy, instead choosing to use bluff, bluster and intimidation to throw his weight around. Everyone in the room already knew that the United States was the 900-pound gorilla, but it had always played nice, choosing to use its strength towards their collective enemies, whomever they were. Now it was more content on shaking down allies and threatening withdrawal from major treaties, some of which he did do.

Yes, burden-sharing is important. But we need a richer conception of burden-sharing than arbitrary funding targets or cutting the margins of trading partners. A new American exceptionalism would shift from absorbing the lion's share of the costs to distributing them more fairly. This does not mean less leadership but rather a different kind of leadership, giving others a greater voice along with greater accountability. The U.S. knows how to do this. Building institutions to spread responsibility for shared problems is part of America's DNA. And on the global stage, institution-building enhances American power and effectiveness.

The second key attribute of American exceptionalism is a can-do spirit. We live in a country full of problem-solvers, in a world full of problems. The historian Frederick Jackson Turner's famous "frontier thesis" described Americans as having a "practical, inventive turn of mind, quick to find expedients." For the past 70 years, a habit of problem-solving has defined America's role in the world.

I saw this problem-solving streak at every level of government, including the very top. Once, during climate-change negotiations in Copenhagen, in December 2009, heads of state met in a tiny room until 2 o'clock in the morning. When the meeting finally broke up, a blizzard was raging outside. Only a single motorcade could pull up at a time. The result was a bizarre taxi line: world leaders queuing in a Danish conference center in the middle of the night, waiting for their cars to arrive. Eventually, Nicolas Sarkozy, then the president of France, stepped forward and shouted, "I want to die!" But President Obama and Secretary of State Clinton were energized. They raced around the conference center the next day, twisting arms and ultimately salvaging the Copenhagen Accord, which, while flawed and incomplete, helped pave the way for the 2015 Paris Agreement. By the time Obama left office, he had reached an unequivocal conclusion: "If we don't set the agenda, it doesn't happen."

America's can-do approach is sometimes naive. It often fails to come to terms with structural causes or foundational flaws. The U.S. is better at addressing the poor quality of roads around Kabul (which officials know how to fix) than regime rot and corruption (which they do not know how to fix). Even so, at a time when solutions to global problems demand cooperation among governments and the private sector—including faith communities and philanthropies, mayors and activists—the U.S. possesses the creativity and boldness required to assemble unlikely coalitions.

Some people will not unreasonably ask why, if America is any good at problem-solving, the world is such a mess. U.S. foreign policy has certainly failed to solve a lot of problems, and created more than a few. These skeptics are operating from the wrong baseline, though. A nation's foreign policy is the total of imperfect decisions made by imperfect people facing imperfect choices with imperfect information. Mistakes are inevitable, and even successes beget new problems.

This is not to say that there isn't considerable room for improvement, especially when it comes to setting priorities. Americans may like to solve problems, but which problems should they be trying to solve? The answer cannot be all of them, everywhere. As the Harvard economist Michael Porter has pointed out, "The essence of strategy is choosing what not to do." America's priorities should consist of the list I outlined earlier—challenges that legitimately threaten its way of life. Americans should throw every ounce of their problem-solving weight against those threats.

Even with clearer priorities, the U.S. needs to adopt the foreign-policy version of the serenity prayer: Grant us the wisdom to know the difference between those things we can change and those we cannot. Too often, the U.S. succumbs to the temptation to go toe-to-toe with adversaries in situations where they have an advantage. For example, when the Chinese military started building on rocks and reefs in the South China Sea, the U.S. jumped up and down even though it could do little to stop the construction short of using military force, which it was not prepared to do. The U.S. ended up looking weak. Worse, it let the measure of success become something other than its vital interest, which is not those rocks and reefs. Its vital interest is the freedom of navigation for commercial and military ships. The U.S. can enforce that interest by increasing naval operations in the area and getting its partners to do the same, demonstrating that the world rejects China's claims to these waters and forcing Beijing to decide whether to stop us. Sometimes, the answer is not to try to solve the problem created by others, but rather to make others contend with realities created for them. This was what Truman was up to with the Berlin airlift, which then–Secretary of State Dean Acheson later wrote "gave the Russians the choice of either not interfering or of initiating an air attack, which might have brought upon them a devastating response."

Finally, the relationship between America's interests at home and its interests abroad must always be kept in mind. Obama, listening to his national-security team ask for more money for Afghanistan, would shake his head and point out that he was the only person in the room who had to think about all the things we were not spending money on at home. This should not be about guns versus butter, but about what will position America to compete effectively—especially with China, which is now poised to out-invest the U.S. in technological innovation and R&D.

It should also be about where the middle class fits into America's foreign-policy priorities. The erosion of America's middle class is sapping the nation's strength. The main causes lie in domestic policy, but foreign policy bears responsibility as well.

During the Obama administration, when the national-security team sat around the Situation Room table, we rarely posed the question What will this mean for the middle class? Many other countries have made economic growth that expands the middle class a key organizing principle of their foreign policy. The American people want their leaders to do the same: to focus on how strength abroad can contribute to a strong economic foundation at home, and not just vice versa.

And they're right. The country's entire national-security strategy, the resources it allocates, the threats and opportunities it prioritizes, the events and circumstances it tries to shape, the relationships it cultivates, should more explicitly be geared toward reviving America's middle class. As a starting point, the U.S. must define what counts as its "economic interest," looking beyond generic GDP growth in order to understand the impact of specific policies on corporations and communities. Who are the real winners and losers? When we negotiated some new development in a foreign land and we later learned that the company planned to import materials from other countries, not the United States. Whose interests, exactly, were we serving? Whose interests are we serving by putting diplomatic muscle into helping companies like Walmart open stores in India?

America's trade and investment strategies should place less emphasis on making the world safe for corporate investment and more emphasis on international tax and anti-corruption policies that target drivers of inequality. Jennifer Harris, a former State Department colleague, posed an arresting question asked recently: How is it that the domestic economic agenda of the Obama administration could be so different in its values and priorities from President George W. Bush's, so much more focused on the needs of working people, while its international economic agenda was nearly identical? The answer is that both political parties came to treat international economic issues as somehow separate from everything else. U.S. internationalism became insufficiently attentive to the needs and aspirations of the American middle class. Changing that is a prerequisite of an effective and sustainable foreign policy that enhances the American way of life.

A third attribute of America's exceptional role is that the country is more willing than other advanced democracies to wield power in all forms. This is in no small part because Americans see themselves (rightly or wrongly) not as choosing to act but rather as called to act, by circumstances or by other nations.

Dick Cheney's approach revolved almost exclusively around hard power: F-35s, battleships, tanks. Donald Trump has exacerbated this problem, boosting the military's budget while depleting the diplomatic corps. A new American exceptionalism would recognize that the country's durable power comes from creative, credible, and tenacious diplomacy backed by the threat of force, not force backed by the eventual hope of diplomacy.

First, the U.S. has to wind down its participation in the forever wars of the Middle East. This doesn't mean abandoning the region or shutting down the counterterrorism mission. But it does mean finally bringing the war in Afghanistan, which has now gone on for more time than any other war in American history, to a responsible close. Military engagement in other parts of the region needs stricter limits. The blank check for military action that Congress gave the president in 2001 should be transformed into a much narrower authorization, one that excludes participation in counterproductive missions, such as the ongoing one in Yemen, whose only clear outcome is a humanitarian crisis.

In addition, the U.S. should rebalance its priorities among the various forms of American power—defense, diplomacy, development, trade, investment, and technology. One idea is to group them all into a unified national-security budget, which would allow for shifting money from outdated military systems and bloated line items to, say, investments in artificial intelligence and resilient infrastructure. Building that budget requires asking hard questions. For example, the U.S. has historically been the least vulnerable nation in the world, thanks to the Atlantic and Pacific Oceans; are enough resources going into a strategy to deal with the fact that, in cyberspace, it is now among the most vulnerable? And in the strategic competition with China, is the United States underweighted on the military dimension or in the realm of technology and economics?

Finally, the U.S. must get better at seeing both the possibilities and the limits of American power. and match its means to its stated ends. As Walter Lippmann observed, "In foreign relations, as in all other relations, a policy has been formed only when commitments and power have been brought into balance."

Syria is a tragic case of the means-ends gap. The American president declared that the Syrian leader, Bashar al-Assad, had to go, but the United States didn't make that happen. Hundreds of thousands of people were slaughtered, millions fled the country, and a civil war continues to rage. As a participant in many of the debates about whether to intervene, I have struggled to determine where we went wrong. My tentative conclusion is that we should have done more to try to achieve less. Those of us who advocated for using substantial American means in Syria also argued for maximalist ends (a swift transition to a new government in Damascus) that proved unachievable. Meanwhile, those who advocated for more limited objectives also argued that we should use very modest means, or not get involved at all. Nobody was arguing to both increase the means (more and earlier pressure on Assad) and temper the ends (give up the demand that Assad leave and focus instead on curbing his worst behavior). That would not have solved the deeper problem, but it might have reduced the overall level of violence, death, and displacement, and set the stage for a better long-term outcome.

The fourth and final attribute emerges from a historical fact: The United States was fashioned not from a territory or tribe but from a set of ideas. The Founders proclaimed the values of liberty and equality. They established the supremacy of "We the People." Although their worldview incorporated racist and sexist elements, the legacy of which continues to roil American society today, they also anticipated progress toward "a more perfect union." Establishing a state based on ideas was itself exceptional. Europeans pursued independence based on nationality: as Czechs, Poles, Hungarians, Ukrainians, Lithuanians. America's story is different.

Crucially, the Founders believed not just in individual rights but in the common good. They were not small-d democrats but rather small-r republicans. They embraced the notion of interdependence—that human beings have shared interests and need institutions to pursue those interests, and that liberty can be preserved only through such institutions. They believed that a good society is the product of active citizenship combined with responsible and virtuous leadership. And they viewed these truths as universal—the United States was not coming into existence to rise and fall as other powers had, but rather to transform the world.

The United States cannot expect to lead if it is offering only pragmatism, and not aspiration.

These founding principles coalesced into an American creed, which eventually served as the basis for the country's postwar influence abroad. But in recent decades, that foundation has cracked. Many (mostly white) Americans are looking not to the nation's founding ideas but to Donald Trump's very unexceptional version of nationalism as a channel for their frustrations and hopes. America's friends are taking note of the divisions, while its competitors are exploiting them. Franklin D. Roosevelt once spoke of the United States as an "arsenal of democracy"; today, an arsenal of autocracy is forming as authoritarian states seek to put pressure on America's political and economic model.

The current moment calls for a new form of patriotism—for citizens of all political stripes to embrace a sense of national pride based on America's founding ideas. In the current climate, this is a task of daunting proportions. But I believe that most people are eager for an inclusive and welcoming patriotic spirit—one that, as the historian Jefferson Cowie put it, refuses to surrender the American story "to the voices of exclusion and avarice." Winning this battle will require enormous work at home, where much of the emphasis must lie.

It will also require a renewed belief in the power of American values in the world. I can imagine two types of readers rolling their eyes. One group will ask why we should make values a priority at all, rather than simply securing our interests. But as the late John McCain once noted, "It is foolish to view reason and idealism as incompatible or to consider our power and wealth as encumbered by the demands of justice, morality, and conscience." A place for values in the conduct of foreign policy is built into the character of a country founded on ideas. It is also essential to our interests, because freer, less corrupt, more open societies are less likely to threaten America's way of life. Moreover, the U.S. cannot expect to lead if it is offering only pragmatism, and not aspiration. It can't necessarily outbid China, which has much more cash to spend abroad, but it can out-persuade and out-inspire.

The other group will call out the many times that the United States has not acted on its asserted ideals. The theologian Reinhold Niebuhr reminds us why this will always be so: "Hypocrisy and pretension are the inevitable concomitants of the engagement between morals and politics," he wrote, adding, "They do not arise where no effort is made to bring the power impulse of politics under the control of conscience." American leaders after

Trump do not need to make categorical claims that place values above every other consideration. They should be more honest and more precise, but no less proud. Values have been a genuine consideration in the weighing of interests, and the U.S. has tried far more than other great powers to take them into account. This is rare and impressive enough. Proceeding from this basis, a new American exceptionalism can more consistently, if more modestly, secure a place for values in the conduct of foreign policy.

Some argue that the United States is fractured beyond repair—that Donald Trump is destroying American credibility and, with it, all possibility of renewed American leadership. Some also contend that you can no longer make arguments to the American people based on higher purpose—they are too angry or too cynical.

I see it another way. Let's not forget that, throughout American history, the path forward has been determined not in times of disruption but in their aftermath. The New Deal followed the Great Depression, just as the Marshall Plan followed the Second World War. When Donald Trump exits the White House, the United States will once again have a chance to chart a new course. Its friends will not give up on the country in the interim, at least not until the next election clarifies whether Washington's abdication is the work of a rogue president or the will of the country. They want to be America's partners. As for the American people, I believe that they would welcome a renewed form of exceptionalism that addresses their concerns, speaks to their aspirations, and restores confidence that their country can be a force for good in the world.

America as a force for good in the world, who talks like that anymore? Is this all just the "gaudy mumbo jumbo of politicians," as Robert Hayden put it in his poem "Frederick Douglass"? Well, I believe we should talk like this. Our greatest leaders through history talked like this. And America's most principled critics, like Douglass himself, have been among its greatest patriots. They understood, as we must, that American exceptionalism is not a description of reality but the expression of an ambition. It is about striving, and falling short, and improving. This is the essence of a patriotism that every American can embrace.

Reclaiming America's place in the world will be an extraordinary challenge. For decades, the country neglected needed updates to the international system. Now Donald Trump is blowing that system up. The saying goes that when a natural disaster hits, "build back better." The same applies to foreign policy. Not since 1945 has the U.S. had the chance to go back to basics and decide which parts to keep, which to scrap, and, above all, which to reinvent. After Trump, it can do just that.

Joe Biden paid a visit to Lee Kuan Yew, the former prime minister of Singapore, who expressed admiration for America's famed "black box."

"Black box?" Biden asked.

"You know, the black box that the Americans have buried that contains the secret for how they can constantly reinvent themselves."

We need to find and unlock that black box.

8.

Here we are friends and neighbors, the final chapter. Throughout this book I have presented what I feel is a pretty convincing argument as the why the concept of American Exceptionalism is a myth. And that we were pretty much lied to for our entire lives. Now does that mean we should no longer stand for the National Anthem, salute the flag, say the Pledge of Allegiance, or support our troops? By all means, my response is a resounding "NO!" It is these rituals and traditions which solidify us as a nation, and give us a recognized, national feeling of togetherness. For those of you still not convinced regarding the mythos, I have one question for you, "When was America, at any point in our history, ever great?"

Was it in 1609, when Jamestown was founded, and European settlers brought their diseases to the Native Americans, who had no natural defenses? Was it in 1619, when the first African slaves were brought to America? What about 1620, when the Puritans landed in Plymouth, Massachusetts? They would have starved to death first winter if the Piqua Indians had not shared their food with them, and then in the spring taught them how to plant crops that would allow them to put away stores for the winter? Oh, and the Piqua's reward for helping the Puritans? Almost the entire Piqua nation was slaughtered because the Puritans thought they knew where gold was. How about the French and Indian War? How about the Revolutionary War and the years leading up to it? How about the Whiskey Rebellion, when President George Washington actually lead troops against people who refused to pay the tax on the whiskey they manufactured (which was the only time in American History a sitting President ever did so.) How about during the removal of several Indian tribes during the "Trail of Tears?" What about during the Great American Tragedy otherwise known as The American Civil War or the resulting Reconstruction? What about the Jim Crow era, surely that was a time when American was truly great, right? How about the great Western expansion, when the buffalo were driven to the point of extinction and the Native American nations were slaughtered en masse. Again, we criticized Nazi Germany for their extermination program against Jews, Romas, Gays, Slavs, and a whole host of other "undesirables," yet we as Americans remain strangely silent in regards to our treatment of Blacks and Native Americans over the years. The lynchings of Blacks, destruction of their property, the rounding up of Native Americans to be placed on Reservations, to the current killing of unarmed Black men and women by the police because they "feared for their safety," and then get away with murder gives us all pause to think.

I know you're thinking, "Okay, Dwayne. You got us. Maybe America wasn't as great as we were led to believe. But you still have to admit it is a good nation to grow up." That I couldn't agree with you more. But we could always strive and reach to do better.

We have, within our borders, people going to bed hungry at night. We have people who do not have a safe place to sleep at night. We have people right now who have to make the conscious decision between buying food or buying medicine. We have elected officials who want school children to work as unpaid janitors at their schools so they can eat a school lunch. Granted, I have nothing against hard work, as I was instilled with a work ethic by both my father and grandfather. In my younger days, I could work circles around not only my peers but folks younger than myself. But to suggest that poor children are poor simply because they are lazy ignores a key aspect of Capitalism. Capitalism does not distribute resources or rewards equally, with few winners and a lot of losers. If it was not for those in the lower classes, those in the wealthier classes could not or would not be able to function because they would have no one to provide services to them.

One thing we, as Americans are going to relearn to do is the fine art of compromise. As it currently stands, compromise is a dirty word in the political climate of today. Each side digs in with their positions and plays a war of attrition on the nightly news, with usually those in the majority getting what they want with barely any consideration of the rights of the minority. Once upon a time in this country, politicians actually practiced to art of both compromise and negotiations, where meeting somewhere in the middle was the preferred method of governance, instead of these constant games of political one-upmanship.

And, back in the day, we did not have these consulting firms and news outlets which filled the airwaves with enough bullshit to fertilize a wheatfield. They take things said out of context and vilify any progressive idea as socialistic. The problem is their target audience can barely spell the word socialist, let alone give you the correct or a concrete definition of the word. For that I fault the public education system for their failure to adequately teach the populous about what laws mean what and what our founding documents really say. Very few people can tell you what five rights are granted in the First Amendment, and only one half of the Second Amendment. They probably couldn't tell you anything about Amendments 3 – 9, they might be able to discuss Amendment 10, and avoid like the plague Amendments 13 and 14, and have no clue about the rest of the Amendments to the Constitution. This is what most learned people are faced with when having a discussion with their uncle over Thanksgiving dinner. Having a battle of wits with an unarmed man.

Is this the America in which we want to live? A nation of endless election cycles, political advertising, TV networks telling us how to think by playing to our deepest fears? I'm not satisfied with the level of political ignorance in this country. Instead of having an informed electorate, we usually have two groups, each isolated to themselves, in their own corresponding echo chambers, only hearing what they want to hear and getting reflected back upon them their own thoughts. This has got to stop. Donald Trump was a wake-up call for all of us, both on the right and left, instead of viewing him as the Savior of this nation or the Anti-Christ, let's view him as he really is, an opportunist. A businessman who sensed the division of the American people and took full advantage of it. An expert in marketing his brand, he appeals to the lowest common denominator in us. He played on our collective hopes and fears. He put forth his business experience as an asset where he was not "just another politician," and the Democrats did not help matters any by fielding one of the weakest candidates they could have because, "it was her turn."

Senators Bernie Sanders (I-VT) and Congresswoman Alexandria Ocasio-Cortez (D-NY) are now calling the shots in the progressive wing of the Democratic Party. They are smart, have excellent ideas and if they gain enough traction could be able to provide the United States with some much-needed progressive legislation. Things such as Medicare for All, Free College for all. These two items would go a long way in addressing two of the greatest hurdles within the American economic system, freeing up money for much needed other expenditures. So why are so many people against the progressive agenda, you might ask? Actually, it is rather simple to explain. Most Americans work hard, but never hard enough to qualify to make enough to what is called "the big bucks." Most folks can only can afford health insurance only through their employers, if they are self-employed or have lost their jobs, their options are limited and quite expensive. The same with a college education, it has been priced out of the reach of lower- and middle-class student without benefit of some type of student loan. These saddle the student with a heavy debt burden which hinders them from obtaining a mortgage or any other type of debt.

So now comes the $64,000 question, how do we make America great? One way is for all of us to pull together on the important issues. Will we continue to have our minor skirmishes over nuts-

and-bolts issues within our Republic? Of course, we will that is what makes our country different than so many others. That we can agree to disagree and still attend school, church and work together.

Look at it like this, we on the left are not true socialists, we are left-center on the grand political spectrum. You on the right? While you would like to think of yourself as some kind of New Age Fascists, barely are center-left. In other words, the difference between the right and left wings in this country is so slim, one could barely slide a piece of paper between us. No one is advocating armed taking of private property or open warfare in the streets, come on. Americans are way too soft to go advocating for bloodshed, especially if it is their own blood which might get shed.

Folks on the Right, listen up. No liberal openly advocates for the wholesale slaughter of babies, okay? What we do advocate for is the right for a woman to make her own decisions governing her own health, ALL OF HER HEALTH, which includes reproductive health. You do not see the government want to regulate the sale of Viagra or the need for a prostate exam, do you? We don't want to take your guns, but the denationalization of the mentally ill, some check has to be put into place to keep firearms out of those hands who have been deemed by our judicial system as severely mentally ill. And yes, we do advocate the raising of taxes, particularly the top marginal tax rates. As I might have mentioned before, during the 1950's the top marginal tax rate was 90%, from 1963 to 1980, the top marginal tax rate was 70%. This was only on the top wage earners in the country. During this time, we built the interstate highway system, schools, roads, bridges, a space program, and many other things which made us a shining example throughout the world. Oh, and we even balanced the Federal budget in 1959, Eisenhower being the only Republican in history to do so.

Now, with our top marginal tax rate is 27%, suddenly we no

longer have the money to even repair or even upkeep what infrastructure we do have. Of course, the Republican party's solution to everything is privatization. I suppose folks would really love the return of turnpikes and toll roads in their daily commutes. While the private sector is good at doing somethings well, they are driven by the profit motive. Which means that they would have free reign to charge as much as the market would bear for their product or service. Is that they type of country you'd really like to live? Or would you just shrug your shoulders and say, "Oh well," and pay up.

We can and do deserve better.

Our society can be great, but it takes far more than just talk and rhetoric. It takes more than just practicing verbal vomit over what one hears on Fox News or CNN. It takes more than just sitting in an echo chamber of friends and associates who view the world as you do. And it definitely takes more than having all your friends and associates being of the same socio-economic background or race that you belong. Hint: that is the same as being in an echo chamber.

My assessment: We'll be alright, just as soon as we realize there is more that binds us than divides us. I am hoping these last four years under Trump as our leader has taught us how we are very easily manipulated into see our neighbors or even other family members as the enemy. And how badly some of us need to look up both the definition of the word "socialist," and study a true political science spectrum of political philosophies. The wounds he has inflicted upon the American body politic are deep and will take time to heal, but heal they shall. And it will leave a rather nasty scar that will always be with us for the rest of history. History will not be kind to Donald J. Trump, not only because of the damage he inflicted upon our Republic, but also, he continued carrying forward the mythos of American Exceptionalism.

WORKS CITED

Winfried Fluck; Donald E. Pease; John Carlos Rowe (2011). Reframing the Transnational Turn in American Studies. University Press of New England. p. 207. ISBN 9781611681901.

American Exceptionalism: A Double-Edged Sword. Seymour Martin Lipset. New York, N.Y.: W.W. Norton & Co., Inc. 1996. p. 18.

Seymour Martin Lipset, The first new nation (1963).

Lipset, American Exceptionalism, pp. 1, 17–19, 165–74, 197

de Tocqueville, Alexis. Democracy in America (1840), part 2, p. 36: "The position of the Americans is therefore quite exceptional, and it may be believed that no other democratic people will ever be placed in a similar one."

Tyrrell, Ian (October 21, 2016). "What, exactly, is 'American exceptionalism'?". The Week.

Eldon Eisenach, "A Progressive Conundrum: Federal Constitution, National State, and Popular Sovereignty" in Stephen Skowronek et al., eds., The Progressives' Century: Political Reform, Constitutional Government, and the Modern American State (Yale University Press, 2016) pp 29-30.

Zimmer, Ben (September 27, 2013). "Did Stalin Really Coin "American Exceptionalism"?". Slate.com.

Albert Fried, Communism in America: A History in Documents (1997), p. 7.

Donald E. Pease (2009). The New American Exceptionalism. U of

Minnesota Press. p. 10. ISBN 978-0-8166-2782-0.

Rose, Richard (1989). "How Exceptional is the American Political Economy?". Political Science Quarterly. 104 (1): 91–115. doi:10.2307/2150989. JSTOR 2150989.

David W. Noble, Death of a Nation: American Culture and the end of exceptionalism, pp. xxiii ff.

Timothy Roberts and Lindsay DiCuirci, eds., American Exceptionalism (2013) vol. 1, p. 9

Michael Kammen and Stanley N. Katz. "Bernard Bailyn, Historian, and Teacher: An Appreciation." in James A. Henretta, Michael Kämmen, and Stanley N. Katz, eds. The Transformation of Early American History: Society, Authority, and Ideology (1991) p. 10.

Bernard Bailyn, The Ideological Origins of the American Revolution. p. 92

Pease, Donald E. (2009). The New American Exceptionalism. U of Minnesota Press. p. 10. ISBN 978-0-8166-2783-7.

How Joseph Stalin Invented American Exceptionalism, The Atlantic.

Iviea, Robert L.; Ginerb, Oscar (2009). "American Exceptionalism in a Democratic Idiom: Transacting the Mythos of Change in the 2008 Presidential Campaign". Communication Studies. 60 (4): 359–75. doi:10.1080/10510970903109961. S2CID 143578350.

"Foreword: on American Exceptionalism; Symposium on Treaties, Enforcement, and U.S. Sovereignty", Stanford Law Review, May 1, 2003, p. 1479

Alexis de Tocqueville, Democracy in America, Vintage Books, 1945

"Manifest Destiny". Encyclopaedia Britannica.

Kammen p. 7

Quentin R. Skrabec (2009). William McGuffey: Mentor to American Industry. Algora Publishing. p. 223. ISBN 978-0-87586-728-1.

Fried, Albert. Communism in America: a history in documents, pp. 7–8, 19, 82–92. Columbia University Press, 1997. ISBN 0-231-10235-6

Pease, Donald E. Editors: Bruce Burgett and Glenn Hendler. "Exceptionalism", pp. 108–12, in "Keywords for American Cultural Studies. NYU Press, 2007. ISBN 0-8147-9948-5

Edwards, Brian T.; Gaonkar, Dilip Parameshwar (2010). Globalizing American Studies. University of Chicago Press. pp. 58–59. ISBN 978-0-226-18507-1.

McCoy, Terrence (March 15, 2012). "How Joseph Stalin Invented 'American Exceptionalism'". The Atlantic, March 15, 2012. Retrieved September 13, 2013.

Johnpoll, Bernard K. A Documentary History of the Communist Party of the United States. Vol. II, Vol. II. Westport, Conn: Greenwood Press, 1994, p. 196.

Dorothy Ross (1991). Origins of American Social Science. p. 23.

Dorothy Ross (1991). Origins of American Social Science. pp. 24–25.

Smith, Henry Nash (Spring 1950). "The Frontier Hypothesis and the Myth of the West". American Quarterly. 2 (1): 3–11. doi:10.2307/2710571. JSTOR 2710571.

Dorothy Ross (1991). Origins of American Social Science. p. 25.

American Exceptionalism. The Washington Post

Dick Cheney and Liz Cheney (2015). Exceptional: Why the World Needs a Powerful America. Simon & Schuster. ISBN

9781442388314. Retrieved November 3, 2015.

Holland, Catherine A. (2005). "Hartz and Minds: The Liberal Tradition after the Cold War". Studies in American Political Development. 19 (2): 227–33. doi:10.1017/S0898588X05000155.

Cross, Gary (1995). "Comparative Exceptionalism: Rethinking the Hartz Thesis in the Settler Societies of Nineteenth-Century United States and Australia". Australasian Journal of American Studies. 14 (1): 15–41. JSTOR 41053761.

Anna Gandziarowski, The Puritan Legacy to American Politics (2010) p. 2

Justin B. Litke, "Varieties of American Exceptionalism: Why John Winthrop Is No Imperialist," Journal of Church and State, 54 (Spring 2012), 197–213.

The Hanover Historical Texts Project, ed. (August 1996). "John Winthrop, A Modell of Christian Charity (1630)". Collections of the Massachusetts Historical Society (Boston, 1838), 3rd series 7:31–48. Archived from the original on April 13, 2010. Retrieved March 13, 2010.

Sarah Rivett, "Religious Exceptionalism and American Literary History: 'The Puritan Origins of the American Self' in 2012." Early American Literature 7.2 (2012): 391-410.

"Chapter posting" (PDF). www.socialjudgments.com.

Schultz, Kevin M. (January 15, 2013). Tri-Faith America: How Catholics and Jews Held Postwar America to Its Protestant Promise. Oxford University Press. ISBN 9780199987542 – via Google Books.

Gordon Wood, "Introduction" in Idea of America: Reflections on the Birth of the United States (2011) online.

Gordon S. Wood (2009). The Purpose of the Past: Reflections on the Uses of History. Penguin. p. 240. ISBN 9781440637919.

Hoogenboom, Ari (2002). "American Exceptionalism Republicanism as Ideology". In Gläser, Elisabeth; Wellenreuther, Hermann (eds.). Bridging the Atlantic: the question of American exceptionalism in perspective. pp. 43–67. ISBN 978-0-521-78205-0.

Kidd, Thomas S. (2010). God of Liberty: A Religious History of the American Revolution. New York: Basic Books. p. 9. ISBN 978-0-465-00235-1.

Kidd, God of Liberty, p. 8

Tucker, Robert W.; Hendrickson, David C. (1992). Empire of Liberty: The Statecraft of Thomas Jefferson. p. ix. ISBN 9780198022763.

Quoted in Tucker and Hendrickson, Empire of Liberty p. 7; see John P. Foley, ed. The Jeffersonian Cyclopedia (1900) text p. 895

Marilyn B. Young, "One Empire Under G", European Contributions to American Studies, May 2004, Vol. 55, pp. 8–18

Larry Schweikart and Dave Dougherty, A Patriot's History of the Modern World, From America's Exceptional Ascent to the Atomic Bomb, 1898–1945. Sentinel. ISBN 978-1-59523-089-8. Moreover, A Patriot's History of the Modern World, Vol. II, From the Cold War to the Age of Entitlement, 1945–2012. Sentinel. ISBN 978-1-59523-104-8

Cheney, Dick and Liz Cheney. Exceptional: Why the World Needs a Powerful America, Threshold Editions, New York, 2015. pp. 259ff. ISBN 978-1-5011-1541-7.

Williams, T. Harry (June 1953). "Abraham Lincoln – Principle and Pragmatism in Politics: A Review Article". Mississippi Valley Historical Review. 40 (1): 97. doi:10.2307/1897545. JSTOR 1897545.

Robert Alan Dahl (1997). Toward democracy--a journey: reflections, 1940–1997. Institute of Governmental Studies Press, University of California, Berkeley. p. 2:711. ISBN 9780877723721.

Eric Foner, "Birthright Citizenship Is the Good Kind of American Exceptionalism," The Nation Aug. 27, 2015

Harold Hongju Koh, "On American Exceptionalism" 55 Stan. L. Rev. 1479 (2003) quote at p. 1487 online

Exceptional: Why the World Needs a Powerful America, By Dick Cheney and Liz Cheney. Simon & Schuster. September 2015. ISBN 9781442388314. Retrieved October 5, 2015.

Richard W. Etulain, Does the Frontier Experience Make America Exceptional? (1999)

Walker D. Wyman and Clifton B. Kroeber, eds. Frontier in Perspective (1957)

Marvin K. Mikesell, "Comparative Studies in Frontier History," in Richard Hofstadter and Seymour Martin Lipset, eds., Turner and the Sociology of the Frontier (1968) pp. 152–72

Carroll, Dennis (1982). "Mateship and Individualism in Modern Australian Drama". Theatre Journal. 34 (4): 467–80. doi:10.2307/3206809. JSTOR 3206809.

Kaelble, Hartmut (1981). Social Mobility in the Nineteenth and Twentieth Centuries: Europe and America in Comparative Perspective. New York: Columbia University Press. ISBN 978-0-231-05274-0.

Thernstrom, Stephan (1999). The Other Bostonians: Poverty and Progress in the American Metropolis, 1880–1970. Cambridge: Harvard University Press. ISBN 978-1-58348-443-2.

Stephenson, Charles; Jensen, Richard; Webster, Janice Reiff (1978). Social predictors of American mobility: a census capture-recapture study of New York and Wisconsin, 1875–1905. Newberry Library.

Blau, Peter M.; Duncan, Otis Dudley (1978). The American Occupational Structure. London: Collier Macmillan. ISBN 978-0-02-903670-9.

De Grauwe, Paul (July 2, 2007). "Structural rigidities in the US and Europe". Retrieved January 1, 2010.

Mankiw, Greg (January 12, 2011). "Half-Full Glass of Economic Mobility" (blog). Archived from the original on January 22, 2011. Retrieved January 1, 2011.

Rose, "How Exceptional is the American Political Economy?" Political Science Quarterly (1989) 104#1 pp. 91, 92 in JSTOR

Michael Kamman, "The Problem of American Exceptionalism" American Quarterly (1993) p. 11 [1]

Kamman, "The Problem of American Exceptionalism" p. 12

Kamman, "The Problem of American Exceptionalism" pp. 12–13

Kamman, "The Problem of American Exceptionalism" pp. 12–14

Michael Ignatieff (2009). American Exceptionalism and Human Rights. pp. 3–8. ISBN 978-1400826889.

Charles Philippe David, David Grondin (2006), Hegemony or Empire?: The Redefinition of US Power Under George W. Bush, ISBN 978-0754647744

Frel, Jan (July 10, 2006). "Could Bush Be Prosecuted for War Crimes?". AlterNet. Archived from the original on May 13, 2008. Retrieved May 17, 2008.

Thimm, Johannes. "American Exceptionalism – Conceptual Thoughts and Empirical Evidence" (PDF). Berlin. Archived from the original (PDF) on February 25, 2009. Retrieved October 29, 2013.

Vladimir Putin's comments on American exceptionalism, Syria

cause a fuss. CNN. 12 September 2013. Retrieved 12 September 2013.

"Ecuador's Correa: Obama's exceptionalism talk reminiscent of Nazi rhetoric before WWII". RT. October 4, 2013. Retrieved October 7, 2013.

Zinn, Howard (1980). A People's History of the United States: 1492 to Present. Harper & Row.

Howard Zinn. "The Myth of American Exceptionalism". Archived from the original on October 16, 2007. Retrieved October 21, 2007.

Pease, Donald E. (2009). The New American Exceptionalism. University of Minnesota Press.

Edwards, Mark (2009). "'God Has Chosen Us': Re-Membering Christian Realism, Rescuing Christendom, and the Contest of Responsibilities during the Cold War". Diplomatic History. 33 (1): 67–94. doi:10.1111/j.1467-7709.2008.00747.x.

"Index of /wp". Gilderlehrman.org. Retrieved March 11, 2010.

Reichard, Gary W.; Ted Dickson. America on the World Stage, University of Illinois Press, 2008, back cover. ISBN 0-252-07552-8

Cohen, Roger (September 24, 2008). "Roger Cohen: Palin's American exception". International Herald Tribune. Retrieved December 30, 2011.

Koh, Harold Hongju (May 2003). "Foreword: On American Exceptionalism". Stanford Law Review. The Board of Trustees of Leland Stanford Junior University. Archived from the original on September 11, 2006. Retrieved March 11, 2010.

"Book review: The Myth of American Exceptionalism". The Atlantic. March 18, 2009. Retrieved March 11, 2010.

Hirsh, Michael (January 21, 2009). "No Time to Go Wobbly,

Barack". Washingtonmonthly.com. Archived from the original on October 3, 2009. Retrieved March 11, 2010.

"Americanism, Then and Now: Our Pet Heresy". Catholic Culture. Retrieved March 11, 2010.

"The Heresy of Americanism: Response to Radical Traditionalists". Bringyou.to. Archived from the original on February 5, 2010. Retrieved March 11, 2010.

"The Phantom Heresy?". West Virginia University. Retrieved December 21, 2010.

McAvoy, Thomas T. (1959). "The Catholic Minority after the Americanist Controversy, 1899–1917". Review of Politics. 21 (1): 53–82. doi:10.1017/s0034670500021975.

"Is the U.S. Still a Dependable Ally?". Hudson Institute. Archived from the original on November 18, 2011. Retrieved November 10, 2011.

"Examining Declinism". HumanEvents.com. Archived from the original on January 25, 2013. Retrieved November 10, 2010.

"Three Centuries of American Declinism". RealClearPolitics. August 27, 2007. Retrieved March 11, 2010.

"The Decline and Fall of Declinism". American.com. Archived from the original on January 29, 2010. Retrieved March 11, 2010.

Zakaria, Fareed, The Post-American World. W. W. Norton & Company. ISBN 978-0-670-08229-2

Lloyd, John (December 20, 2009). "Financial Times". Martian myths that flatter Europe. Retrieved January 1, 2010.

Fernández-Armesto, Felipe. The Americas: A Hemispheric History. New York: Modern Library, 2003. p. 17. Print.

Kirchick, James (April 28, 2009). "Squanderer in chief". Los Angeles Times. Retrieved March 11, 2010.

Sheer, Michael (April 5, 2009). "On European Trip, President Tries to Set a New, Pragmatic Tone". The Washington Post. Retrieved November 8, 2010.

Mitt Romney (2010). No Apology: The Case for American Greatness. Macmillan. p. 29. ISBN 978-1-4299-3960-7.

Martin, Jonathan; Smith, Ben (August 20, 2010). "The New Battle: What It Means to be American".

Karen Tumulty, "American exceptionalism, explained", The Washington Post September 12, 2013

Max Fisher, "Vladimir Putin's New York Times op-ed, annotated and fact-checked", The Washington Post September 12, 2013

Kirchik, James (15 August 2016), "Beware the Hillary Clinton-Loathing, Donald Trump-Loving Useful Idiots of the Left", The Daily Beast.

Schwenninger, Sherle R., Heather Hurlburt, Stephen Kinzer and Juan Cole (24 May 2016), "When Donald Trump Says His Foreign Policy Is 'America First'—What Exactly Does He Mean?", The Nation.

Ostroff, Joseph (May 6, 2013). "Bioshock Infinite - Taking American Exceptionalism to the Extreme". Exclaim!.

"America Resurgent". Republican Party.

Bacevich, Andrew (2008). The Limits of Power: The End of American Exceptionalism. Metropolitan Books. ISBN 978-0-8050-8815-1.

Bender, Thomas (2006). A Nation Among Nations: America's Place in World History. Hill & Wang. ISBN 978-0-8090-9527-8.

Cheney, Dick and Liz Cheney (2015). Exceptional: Why the

World Needs a Powerful America. Threshold Editions. ISBN 978-1-5011-1541-7.

Churchwell, Sarah. Behold, America: The Entangled History of 'America First' and 'the American Dream' (2018). 368 pp. online review

Dollinger, Marc. "American Jewish Liberalism Revisited: Two Perspectives Exceptionalism and Jewish Liberalism". American Jewish History (2002) 90#2 pp. 161+. online at Questia

Dworkin, Ronald W. (1996). The Rise of the Imperial Self. Rowman & Littlefield Publishers. ISBN 978-0-8476-8219-5.

Hilfrich, Fabian (2012). Debating American Exceptionalism: Empire and Democracy in the Wake of the Spanish–American War. Palgrave Macmillan. ISBN 978-0-230-39289-2.

Hodgson, Godfrey (2009). The Myth of American Exceptionalism. Yale University Press. ISBN 978-0-300-12570-2.

Hughes, David. "Unmaking an exception: A critical genealogy of US exceptionalism." Review of International Studies (2015) 41#3 pp. 527–51

Madsen, Deborah L. (1998). American Exceptionalism. University Press of Mississippi. ISBN 978-1-57806-108-2.

Glickstein, Jonathan A. American Exceptionalism, American Anxiety: Wages, Competition, and Degraded Labor in The Antebellum United States (2002)

Ferrie, Joseph P. The End of American Exceptionalism: Mobility in the US Since 1850, Journal of Economic Perspectives (Summer, 2005)

Hellerman, Steven L. and Andrei S. Markovits (2001). Offside: Soccer and American Exceptionalism. Princeton University Press. ISBN 978-0-691-07447-4. online version

Ignatieff, Michael ed. (2005). American Exceptionalism and Human Rights. Princeton University Press. ISBN 978-0-691-11647-1.

Kagan, Robert (2003). Of Paradise and Power: America and Europe in the New World Order. Knopf. ISBN 978-1-4000-4093-3.

Kammen, Michael. "The problem of American exceptionalism: A reconsideration." American Quarterly (1993) 45#1 pp. 1–43. online

Koh, Harold Hongju. "On American Exceptionalism" 55 Stan. L. Rev. 1479 (2003) online

Krugman, Paul (2007). The Conscience of a Liberal. W. W. Norton. ISBN 978-0-393-06069-0.

LeBlanc, Paul and Tim Davenport (eds.), The "American Exceptionalism" of Jay Lovestone and His Comrades, 1929–1940: Dissident Marxism in the United States, Volume 1. Leiden, NL: Brill, 2015.

Lipset, Seymour Martin (1997). American Exceptionalism: A Double-Edged Sword. W. W. Norton & Company. ISBN 978-0-393-31614-8.

Lipset, Seymour Martin. The First New Nation. Basic Books, 1955.

Lipset, Seymour Martin. "Still the Exceptional Nation?" The Wilson Quarterly. 24#1 (2000) pp. 31+ online version

Lloyd, Brian. Left Out: Pragmatism, Exceptionalism, and the Poverty of American Marxism, 1890–1922. Johns Hopkins University Press, 1997.

Noble, David (2002). Death of a Nation: American Culture and the End of Exceptionalism. University of Minnesota Press. ISBN 978-0-8166-4080-5.

Restad, Hilde Eliassen, "Old Paradigms in History Die Hard in Political Science: U.S. Foreign Policy and American Exceptionalism", American Political Thought (Notre Dame), (Spring 2012), 1#1 pp. 53–76.

Ross, Dorothy. Origins of American Social Science. Cambridge University Press, 1991.

Ross, Dorothy. "American Exceptionalism" in A Companion to American Thought. Richard W. Fox and James T. Kloppenberg, eds. London: Blackwell Publishers Inc., 1995: 22–23.

Schuck, Peter H., Wilson, James Q., Eds. Understanding America: The Anatomy of an Exceptional Nation, 704 pp, 2008, ISBN 978-1-58648-561-0

Shafer, Byron E., ed. Is America Different?: A New Look at American Exceptionalism (1991) endorses exceptionalism

Soderlind, Sylvia, and James Taylor Carson, eds. American Exceptionalisms: From Winthrop to Winfrey (State University of New York Press; 2012) 268 pp; essays on the rhetoric of exceptionalism in American history, from John Winthrop's "city upon a hill" to the "war on terror".

Swirski, Peter. American Utopia and Social Engineering in Literature, Social Thought, and Political History. New York, Routledge (2011)

Tilman, Rick. "Thorstein Veblen's Views on American 'Exceptionalism': An Interpretation". Journal of Economic Issues. 39#1 2005. pp. 177+. online version

Tomes, Robert. "American Exceptionalism in the Twenty-First Century". "Survival." 56#1. pp. 26–50.

Turner, Frederick Jackson Richard W. Etulain ed. (1999). The Significance of the Frontier in American History, in Does the Frontier Experience Make America Exceptional?.

Tyrrell, Ian. "American Exceptionalism in an Age of International

History", American Historical Review Vol. 96, No. 4 (Oct., 1991), pp. 1031–55 in JSTOR

Voss, Kim. The Making of American Exceptionalism: The Knights of Labor and Class Formation in the Nineteenth Century (1993) online version

Wilentz, Sean. Against Exceptionalism: Class Consciousness and the American Labor Movement, 1790–1820, 26 Int'l Lab. & Working-Class History 1 (1984)

Wrobel, David M. (1996). The End of American Exceptionalism: Frontier Anxiety from The Old West to The New Deal. University Press of Kansas. ISBN 978-0-7006-0561-3.